OLYMPIAD WORKBOOK

NATIONAL CYBER OLYMPIAD

01 **Learning Objectives**

02 **Multiple Choice Questions**

03 **HOTS (Achievers Section)**

04 **Model Test Paper**

05 **Answer Keys and Solutions**

06 **OMR Answer Sheet**

Published by:

V&S PUBLISHERS

F-2/16, Ansari road, Daryaganj, New Delhi-110002
☎ 23240026, 23240027 • *Fax:* 011-23240028
✉ info@vspublishers.com • 🌐 www.vspublishers.com

 **Online Brandstore: amazon.in/vspublishers**

Regional Office : Hyderabad
5-1-707/1, Brij Bhawan (Beside Central Bank of India Lane)
Bank Street, Koti, Hyderabad - 500 095
☎ 040-24737290
✉ vspublishershyd@gmail.com

Follow us on:   

BUY OUR BOOKS FROM: AMAZON FLIPKART

© Copyright: *V&S* PUBLISHERS
ISBN 978-81-978176-4-9
New Edition

DISCLAIMER

PUBLISHER'S NOTE

V&S Publishers has carved a significant niche in the publishing industry over the last decade, having successfully published more than 1000 titles across 9 languages spanning over 50 subject categories. Being known for the quality of content, we have built a reputation of excellence and reliability. We have consistently delivered **"Value & Substance"** to our readers, through a wide range of titles across a variety of genres covering school books, fiction and non-fiction that caters to different people from every section of the society.

The **Olympiad Guidebooks for classes 1-10** across all subjects, launched almost a decade ago, under the **GEN X Imprint**, became a go-to-source for the school students in no time, owing to their invaluable and substantive content written in a guidebook pattern,.

Having successfully sold a million copies of the same and in response to demand by both students as well as shopkeepers nationwide; we now present before you our newly launched **Olympiad Workbook Series**, designed for **classes 1-10 across 4 subjects**.

The workbooks are meticulously curated by a team of experienced educators, researchers and subject matter experts, edited by professionals and peer reviewed by teachers. The team has poured its efforts and expertise into creating a crisp and concise workbook which will help and guide the students to the path of success in Olympiad exams. The **MCQs** identified will not only help in scoring top marks in Olympiads but also inculcate a sense of deeper understanding of the subject, by way of solving **HOTS** and referring to complete solutions at the end of the book.

Here we present our new release– **OLYMPIAD WORKBOOK (NCO) CLASS–6** having following features:

- ☞ Based on the latest syllabi
- ☞ MCQs with comprehensive coverage of topics
- ☞ HOTS Questions liberally included
- ☞ A dedicated chapter on logical reasoning
- ☞ Model test paper for thorough practice
- ☞ Sample OMR sheet for real time simulation

We have made sure through our best efforts, that this workbook strictly follows the latest syllabi and patterns of the Olympiad Examination.

As **V&S Publishers** continuously strive to enhance the readability and maintain the credibility of our academic publications, we seek the support of our valuable readers in influencing and enriching the lives of future generations of students.

P.S. While every care has been taken to ensure the correctness of the content, if you come across any error, howsoever minor, do not hesitate to discuss with teachers while pointing that out to us in no uncertain terms.

We wish you all the best for your exams!

DISTINCTIVE FEATURES

01

Learning Objectives

They list the whole chapter as subtopics, helping the teachers to guide children in a step-by-step manner.

02

Multiple Choice Questions

MCQs act as an excellent learning aid, helping you to understand and work on your mistakes.

03

HOTS (Achievers Section)

The High Order Thinking Questions aim to help the student to solve Application-based questions and gain practical understanding of the subject.

04

Model Test Paper

Model test paper are provided at the end of each book, which help the student to test the knowledge which they have gained after thorough reading of all chapters.

05

Answer Key

Detailed Answer Key along with explanations aid the pupil to indentify, understand the mistakes they make during the course of Olympiad preparation.

CONTENTS

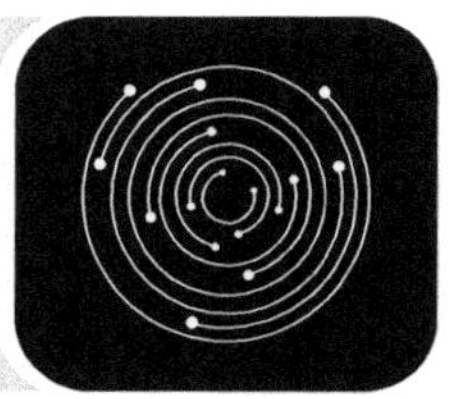

FUNDAMENTALS OF COMPUTER

LEARNING OBJECTIVES

➤ Parts of Personal Computer
➤ Software
➤ Network and Internet

MULTIPLE CHOICE QUESTIONS

1. A computer that connects many other computers and provides access to resources like printers, Internet, files and programs is called ______.
   (A) Mainframe
   (B) Server
   (C) Laptop
   (D) Workstation

2. The main component of a PC which houses the computer's critical parts is called the ______.
   (A) Processor
   (B) Memory
   (C) Cabinet
   (D) System unit

3. The unit of measurement of speed of mainframe computer is ______.
   (A) MIPS
   (B) MBPS
   (C) FLOPS
   (D) TEPS

4. FLOPS stand for ______.
   (A) Flowering Power Operations Per Second
   (B) Following Point Operation Per Second
   (C) Fast Processor Operations Per Second
   (D) Floating Point Operations Per Second

5. Giga TEPS (Traversed Edges Per Second) is the unit of measurement of speed of which type of computer?
   (A) Super computer
   (B) Mini computer
   (C) Micro computer
   (D) Mainframe computer

6. Which of the following computers are primarily used by government organization for critical applications like bulk data processing-like census, consumer statistics?
   (A) Micro computer
   (B) Mini computer
   (C) Mainframe computer
   (D) Super computer

7. PDP-8, the first successful commercial device in its class is an example of a ________.
   (A) Palmtop
   (B) Supercomputer
   (C) Micro computer
   (D) Minicomputer

8. Find the odd one out.
   (A) TI990
   (B) PDP-8
   (C) IBM704
   (D) HP2100 series

9. Commodore 64 is an example of ______.
   (A) Minicomputer
   (B) Microcomputer
   (C) Supercomputer
   (D) Mainframe

10. Microcomputers are also called ______ computers.
    (A) Desktop
    (B) Midrange
    (C) Mimi
    (D) Smart

11. The clock speed of a CPU is measured in ______.
    (A) Gigahertz
    (B) Bits/Bytes per second
    (C) Megahertz
    (D) Both (A) and (C)

12. What is the function of Control Unit in a processor?
    (A) To transfer data to primary storage
    (B) To perform various logical operations
    (C) To store program in memory
    (D) To decode the instruction given by the program

13. When a computer boots up, where are the first instructions to the computer available?
    (A) ROM BIOS
    (B) CPU
    (C) AUTOEXEC
    (D) CONFIG

14. A hard disk platter is divided into tracks. Tracks are further divided into ______.
    (A) Clusters
    (B) Sectors
    (C) Heads
    (D) Ring

15. ______ software directly interacts with the hardware and the ______ software directly interacts with the user.
    (A) Programming System, Operating System
    (B) Interpreter, Operating System
    (C) Application, Operating System
    (D) Operating System, Application

16. Find the odd one out.
    (A) Database Management Software
    (B) Object Code Generation Software
    (C) Word Processing Software
    (D) Desktop Publishing System

17. ______ resides as Firmware within computing and electronic systems.
    (A) Formal software
    (B) Threaded software
    (C) Embedded software
    (D) Mnemonic software

18. A ______ is a computer program that operates or controls a particular device which is attached to the computer.
    (A) Microcode
    (B) Server
    (C) Utility
    (D) Device Driver

19. Which of the following connectors is used to connect a phone line to a modem of a computer?
    (A) RJ-11
    (B) Fire Wire
    (C) RJ-44
    (D) DB-25

20. The application programs that assist the computer by performing house-keeping functions are called ______.
    (A) Assemblers
    (B) Business software
    (C) Spreadsheet programs
    (D) Utility Programs

21. Which of the following storages of a computer system retains information even when the computer switches off or resets?

    (A) Auxiliary storage

    (B) Secondary storage

    (C) Primary storage

    (D) Both (A) and (B)

22. Which of the following statements is correct about the operating system such as Windows 7, Windows 10?

    (A) It is a numeric-analysis tool that allows you to create a kind of computerized ledger.

    (B) It is an entertainment software that allows a computer to be used as an entertainment tool only.

    (C) It is a personal assistance software.

    (D) It takes care of effective and efficient utilization of all hardware and software components of a computer system.

23. Which of the following   s is correct regarding the relationship among hardware, system software, application software and users of a computer system?

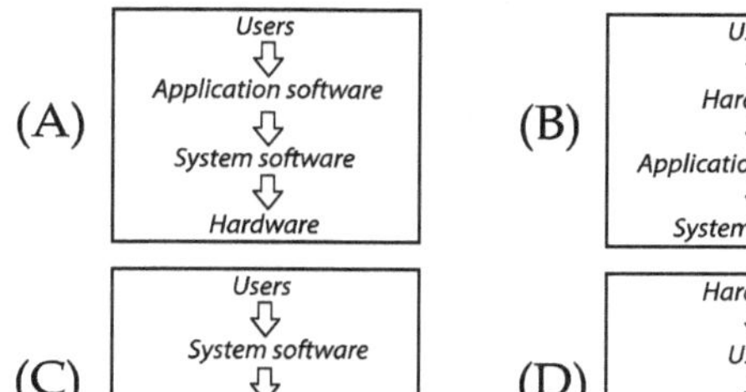

24. Identify the following:

    ■ It is an input device preferred for CAD/CAM applications.

    ■ Designers can move its graphic cursor with hand movements without any movement of equipment.

    ■ It is more suitable to the style of designers.

    (A) Joystick

    (B) Stylus

    (C) Optical mouse

    (D) Trackball

25. Which is the most commonly used video monitor now-a-days?

    (A) Enhance Graphics Array

    (B) Video Graphics Array

    (C) Color Graphics Adapter

    (D) Visual Display Unit

—Darken Your Choice with HB Pencil—

1. Ⓐ Ⓑ Ⓒ Ⓓ	6. Ⓐ Ⓑ Ⓒ Ⓓ	11. Ⓐ Ⓑ Ⓒ Ⓓ	16. Ⓐ Ⓑ Ⓒ Ⓓ	21. Ⓐ Ⓑ Ⓒ Ⓓ
2. Ⓐ Ⓑ Ⓒ Ⓓ	7. Ⓐ Ⓑ Ⓒ Ⓓ	12. Ⓐ Ⓑ Ⓒ Ⓓ	17. Ⓐ Ⓑ Ⓒ Ⓓ	22. Ⓐ Ⓑ Ⓒ Ⓓ
3. Ⓐ Ⓑ Ⓒ Ⓓ	8. Ⓐ Ⓑ Ⓒ Ⓓ	13. Ⓐ Ⓑ Ⓒ Ⓓ	18. Ⓐ Ⓑ Ⓒ Ⓓ	23. Ⓐ Ⓑ Ⓒ Ⓓ
4. Ⓐ Ⓑ Ⓒ Ⓓ	9. Ⓐ Ⓑ Ⓒ Ⓓ	14. Ⓐ Ⓑ Ⓒ Ⓓ	19. Ⓐ Ⓑ Ⓒ Ⓓ	24. Ⓐ Ⓑ Ⓒ Ⓓ
5. Ⓐ Ⓑ Ⓒ Ⓓ	10. Ⓐ Ⓑ Ⓒ Ⓓ	15. Ⓐ Ⓑ Ⓒ Ⓓ	20. Ⓐ Ⓑ Ⓒ Ⓓ	25. Ⓐ Ⓑ Ⓒ Ⓓ

MEMORY AND STORAGE DEVICES

LEARNING OBJECTIVES

➤ Different types of memory and storage devices
➤ Types of storage memory

MULTIPLE CHOICE QUESTIONS

1. A storage device can be __________.
   (A) A built in device that holds information
   (B) The main storage area in a computer which stores data
   (C) An external hardware device used by the computer to store data
   (D) All of these

2. A CD-R is also known as __________.
   (A) WORM
   (B) WORO
   (C) WMRO
   (D) WMRM

3. A secondary storage device is also known as __________.
   (A) Auxiliar
   (B) Main memory
   (C) Available memory
   (D) Primary memory

4. Which of the following is not a secondary storage medium on a computer?

(A) 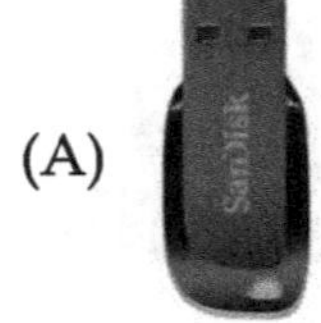

(B) 

(C) 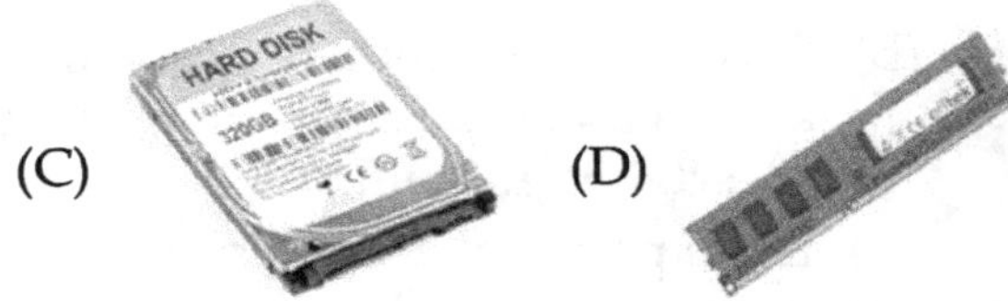

(D)

5. Complete the give diagram by replacing the X, Y and Z with the following Option.

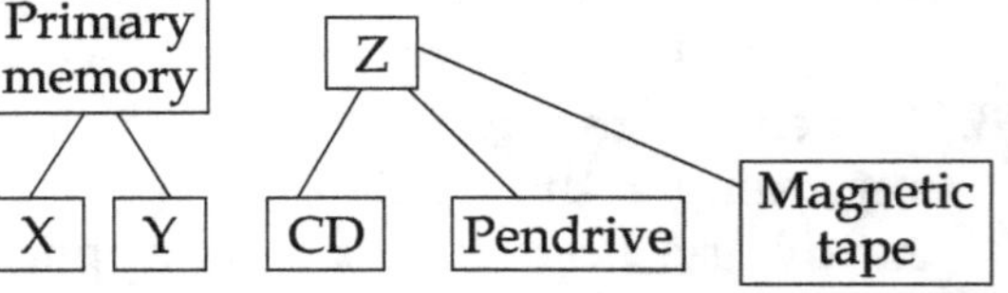

   (A) X - RAM; Y - ROM; Z - Auxiliary memory
   (B) X - RAM; Y - ROM; Z - Secondary memory
   (C) X - Hard disk; Y - RAM; Z - Secondary memory
   (D) Both (A) and (B)

6. I have a document file of 450 MB. I am trying to copy it in a CD-RW. Every time it gives an error message indicating it is unable to copy the file due to some specific reason. What might be the reason?
   (A) A CD-RW cannot hold 450 MB data.
   (B) A CD-RW cannot store documents.

(C) The CD-RW might be having insufficient space.

(D) All the above reasons are possible.

7. Match the following.

Column-I	Column-II
(i) RAM	(a)
(ii) Hard disk drive	(b)
(iii) Floppy	(c)

(A) (i) - (b), (ii) - (c), (iii) - (a)
(B) (i)- (c), (ii) - (a), (iii) - (b)
(C) (i)- (a), (ii) - (c), (iii) - (b)
(D) (i)- (a), (ii) - (b), (iii) - (c)

8. Arrange the following units of memory in decreasing order of their sizes.

Nibble, Terabyte, Zettabyte, Gigabyte, Yottabyte, Bit

(A) Gigabyte > Zettabyte > Terabyte >Yottabyte > Nibble > Bit
(B) Yottabyte > Zettabyte >Gigabyte >Terabyte > Nibble > Bit
(C) Zettabyte > Yottabyte >Terabyte >Gigabyte > Nibble > Bit
(D) Yottabyte > Zettabyte >Terabyte >Gigabyte > Nibble > Bit

9. SATA and PATA are interfaces to connect __________.

(A) Optical drives
(B) Hard disk drives
(C) Magnetic tapes
(D) Both [A] and [B]

10. BIOS of a computer is stored in __________.

(A) RAM
(B) ROM
(C) Cache
(D) Hard Disk

11. What is the difference between Volatile and Non-Volatile Memory?

(A) They are both same types of memory.
(B) Volatile loses its contents when there is no electricity while non-volatile retains its content with or without electricity.
(C) Non-volatile loses its contents when there is no electricity while volatile retains its content with or without electricity.
(D) None of these

12. Which of the following is true?

(A) 4 Nibbles = 1 Byte
(B) 4 Bytes = 1 Nibble
(C) 4 Bits = 1 Nibble
(D) 4 Nibbles = 1 Bit

13. I am having a large video - around 4 GB size which I want to copy from my laptop to my desktop. Which of the following storage medium is best suited for transferring the video to the desktop computer?

(A) 3.5 inch floppy disk
(B) 5.25 inch floppy disk
(C) 8 GB pen drive
(D) A CD ROM which has only around 10 percent space available

14. $(2^{10} \times 2^{10} \times 2^{10})$ Kilo bytes = __________.

(A) 1 Kilobyte
(B) 1 Megabyte
(C) 1 Gigabyte
(D) 1 Terabyte

15. Which of the following memories must be refreshed many times per second?

(A) Static RAM
(B) Dynamic RAM
(C) EEPROM
(D) Flash memory

16. Arrange the following units of memory from the smallest to the largest.

1 nibble, 1 terabyte, 1 byte, 1 petabyte, 1 bit, 1 exabyte

(A) 1 exabyte < 1 petabyte <1 terabyte<1 byte < 1 nibble <1 bit

(B) 1 exabyte <1 petabyte < 1 tera byte< 1 bit < 1 byte < 1 nibble

(C) 1 bit < 1 nibble < 1 byte < 1 terabyte< 1 petabyte < 1 exabyte

(D) 1 bit <1 byte < 1 nibble < 1 exabyte<1 petabyte < 1 terabyte

17. Which of the following hold(s) the CORRECT difference between RAM and ROM?

RAM	ROM
(i) It is a volatile memory	It is a non-volatile memory
(ii) Two main types of RAM are static RAM and Dynamic RAM	Types of ROM include PROM, EPROM and EEPROM
(iii) It allows reading and writing	It only allows reading.

(A) (i) and (ii) only
(B) (ii) and (iii) only
(C) (iii) only
(D) (i), (ii) and (iii)

18. Which of the following statements hold(s) true regarding EEPROM?

Statement 1: It can be reprogrammed and erased by applying special programming signals.

Statement 2: Its full form is Electrically Erasable Programmable Read Only Memory.

(A) Only Statement 1
(B) Only Statement 2
(C) Both Statement 1 and Statement 2
(D) Neither Statement 1 nor Statement 2

19. The place where the data and instruction is stored for a temporarily:

(A) Compact Disc
(B) Hard disc
(C) Memory
(D) None of these

20. Identify the following.

- It uses Integrated Circuit assemblies as memory to store data persistently.
- It has no moving mechanical components and it is typically more resistant to physical shock.

(A) Hard disk drive
(B) Solid-state drive
(C) Magnetic tape drive
(D) All of these

HOTS (ACHIEVERS SECTION)

21. The language of 0's and 1 that computer understands is to be termed as

(A) Numbers
(B) Bits
(C) Codes
(D) Programs

22. The blank chip that uses microcode instructions for programming on a chip.

(A) PROM
(B) EPROM

(C) RAM
(D) None of these

23. The chip that makes uses of ultraviolet technology to erase the contents.

(A) PROM
(B) EEPROM
(C) ROM
(D) EPROM

24. The abbreviation of EPROM is
   (A) Easy for Programming and Read Only Memory
   (B) Early for Program and Readable Only Memory
   (C) Erasable Programmable Read Only Memory
   (D) All of the above

25. This memory helps in improving the processing speed of the computer.
   (A) Cache Memory
   (B) RAM
   (C) ROM
   (D) Flash Memory

1.	Ⓐ Ⓑ Ⓒ Ⓓ	6.	Ⓐ Ⓑ Ⓒ Ⓓ	11.	Ⓐ Ⓑ Ⓒ Ⓓ	16.	Ⓐ Ⓑ Ⓒ Ⓓ	21.	Ⓐ Ⓑ Ⓒ Ⓓ
2.	Ⓐ Ⓑ Ⓒ Ⓓ	7.	Ⓐ Ⓑ Ⓒ Ⓓ	12.	Ⓐ Ⓑ Ⓒ Ⓓ	17.	Ⓐ Ⓑ Ⓒ Ⓓ	22.	Ⓐ Ⓑ Ⓒ Ⓓ
3.	Ⓐ Ⓑ Ⓒ Ⓓ	8.	Ⓐ Ⓑ Ⓒ Ⓓ	13.	Ⓐ Ⓑ Ⓒ Ⓓ	18.	Ⓐ Ⓑ Ⓒ Ⓓ	23.	Ⓐ Ⓑ Ⓒ Ⓓ
4.	Ⓐ Ⓑ Ⓒ Ⓓ	9.	Ⓐ Ⓑ Ⓒ Ⓓ	14.	Ⓐ Ⓑ Ⓒ Ⓓ	19.	Ⓐ Ⓑ Ⓒ Ⓓ	24.	Ⓐ Ⓑ Ⓒ Ⓓ
5.	Ⓐ Ⓑ Ⓒ Ⓓ	10.	Ⓐ Ⓑ Ⓒ Ⓓ	15.	Ⓐ Ⓑ Ⓒ Ⓓ	20.	Ⓐ Ⓑ Ⓒ Ⓓ	25.	Ⓐ Ⓑ Ⓒ Ⓓ

EVOLUTION OF COMPUTER

LEARNING OBJECTIVES

➤ Modern Computers
➤ Generation of Computers

MULTIPLE CHOICE QUESTIONS

1. Which of the following was the 1st calculating device?
   (A) Napier Bones
   (B) Abacus
   (C) Jacquard Loom
   (D) Pascaline

2. Identify the device shown in the picture.

   (A) Analytic Engine
   (B) Jacquard Loom
   (C) Pascaline
   (D) Napier Bones

3. Which one of the following technologies associates itself with the Fourth Generation Computers?
   (A) Artificial Intelligence
   (B) VLSI
   (C) Integrated Circuits
   (D) VALVE

4. LOGO was developed and promoted by _______ as a programming language for young students.
   (A) John Mauchly
   (B) Ada Lovelace
   (C) Seymour
   (D) Bill Gates

5. IBM-704 is associated with which era of computer hierarchy?
   (A) First Generation
   (B) Second Generation
   (C) Third Generation
   (D) Fourth Generation

6. Apple computers were first developed in the 1970s. Who invented the first Apple computers?
   (A) Steve Jobs and Bill Gates
   (B) John von Neumann and Steve Wozniak
   (C) Steve Jobs and Steve Wozniak
   (D) Steve Woznaik and Larry Page

7. The type of computer shown in the figure is _______.

(A) Analog computer
(B) Digital computer
(C) Hybrid computer
(D) Calculating computer

8. Analog and digital signals are processed by which of the following computers?
   (A) Analog Computer
   (B) Digital Computer
   (C) Pascaline
   (D) Hybrid Computer

9. Identify the following:
   - It was a software program.
   - This program was developed in 1993.
   - It was an advance in software development.
   - It was a navigation tool for interactive material.

   (A) Mosaic
   (B) Internet explorer
   (C) Safari
   (D) DOS

10. ______ were used in second generation computers.
    (A) Transistors
    (B) Integrated circuits
    (C) Vacuum tubes
    (D) Microprocessors

11. __________ is an example of second generation computers.
    (A) Microcomputers   (B) EDVAC
    (C) Mark 1   (D) IBM 1401

12. In which years were the second generation computers predominantly found?
    (A) 1980's to present
    (B) 1960's to 1970's
    (C) 1940's to 1950's
    (D) 1950's to 1960's

13. Identify the vital component of the first generation computers shown below.

(A) Integrated Circuits
(B) Silicon Chips
(C) Transistors
(D) Vacuum Tubes

14. Identify the components shown in the picture.

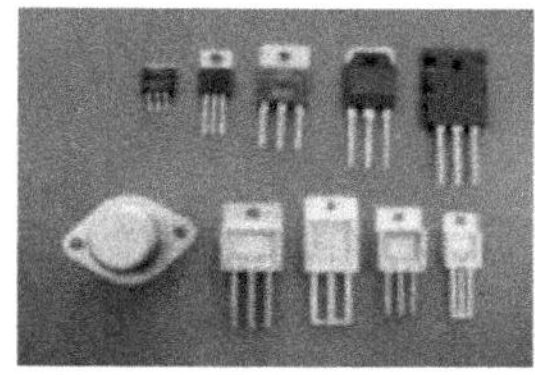

(A) Integrated Circuits
(B) Silicon Chips
(C) Transistors
(D) Vacuum Tubes

15. Which was the electronic general purpose computer in the world?
    (A) UNIVAC
    (B) EDVAC
    (C) PDP-11
    (D) ERA 1101 or UNIVAC 1

16. Which of the following was the first commercially produced computer?
    (A) EDSAC
    (B) ENIAC
    (C) PDP
    (D) ERA1101 or UNIVAC 1

17. Launched in ______, ______ was the world's first minicomputer.
    (A) 1958, PDP-1
    (B) 1960, IBM System/36
    (C) 1961, PDP-11
    (D) 1962, VAX 11/780

18. Match the following.

Column - I	Column - II
(i) Difference Engine	(a) 
(ii) Napier's Bones	(b) 
(iii) Pascaline	(c) 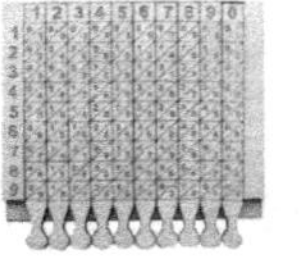
(iv) ENIAC	(d) 

(A) (i)-(d), (ii)-(c), (iii)-(b), (iv)-(a)
(B) (i)-(a), (ii)-(b), (iii)-(c), (iv)-(d)
(C) (i)-(c), (ii)-(d), (iii)-(b), (iv)-(a)
(D) (i)-(c), (ii)-(a), (iii)-(d), (iv)-(b)

19. Match the following.

Column - I	Column - II
(i) 1st Generation Computing Device	(a) Vacuum Tubes
(ii) 1st Generation Computers	(b) ICs
(iii) 2nd Generation Computers	(c) Microprocessor
(iv) 3rd Generation Computers	(d) UNIVAC
(v) 4th Generation Computers	(e) Transistors

(A) (i)-(d), (ii)-(e), (iii)-(a), (iv)-(c), (v)-(b)
(B) (i)-(d), (ii)-(e), (iii)-(a), (iv)-(b), (v)-(c)
(C) (i)-(d), (ii)-(a), (iii)-(e), (iv)-(c), (v)-(b)
(D) (i)-(d), (ii)-(a), (iii)-(e), (iv)-(b), (v)-(c)

20. Which of the following computer is used for nuclear research and similar calculation intensive operations?
(A) Microcomputer
(B) Supercomputer
(C) Minicomputer
(D) Mainframe computer

HOTS (ACHIEVERS SECTION)

21. Which of the following statements is incorrect about fourth generation computers?
(A) They had larger primary and secondary storage capacity as compared to third generation computers.
(B) They were general purpose machines.
(C) Their manufacturing process required manual assembly of individual components into electronic circuits.
(D) They consumed less power than third generation computers.

22. Match the following.

Column-I	Column-II
(i) Honeywell 400	(a) Fourth generation computer
(ii) PARAM	(b) Fifth generation computer
(iii) VAX 9000	(c) Second generation computer

(A) (i) – (c), (ii) – (b), (iii) – (a)
(B) (i) – (a), (ii) – (b), (iii) – (c)
(C) (i) – (b), (ii) – (a), (iii) – (c)
(D) (i) – (c), (ii) – (a), (iii) – (b)

23. What is the key software technology used in fifth generation computers?
   (A) World Wide Web
   (B) Multimedia application
   (C) Internet based application
   (D) All of these

24. Who invented the punch card?
   (A) Charles Babbage
   (B) Semen Korsakov
   (C) Herman Hollerith
   (D) Joseph Marie Jacquard

25. In the late ___________, Herman Hollerith invented data storage on punched cards that could then be read by a machine.
   (A) 1860
   (B) 1900
   (C) 1890
   (D) 1880

WINDOWS 10

4

- ➤ Windows 7 Taskbar
- ➤ Windows 7 Start Menu

MULTIPLE CHOICE QUESTIONS

1. __________ works as primary interface between computer and all programs running on a computer.
   (A) Operating system
   (B) Application software
   (C) Both (A) and (B)
   (D) None of these

2. The time is shown in the _______ area on the taskbar.
   (A) Start menu
   (B) Scrollbar
   (C) Desktop
   (D) Notification of System Tray

3. To open a game like Minesweeper, click _______ > All programs > Games > Minesweeper.

   (A)   (B)

   (C)   (D) Ctrl

4. When you copy a file, Windows places a duplicate copy of the file in the temporary store. The contents of that memory are lost when you shut down the computer. The temporary store used while copying is called _______.

   (A) Program
   (B) Accessibility
   (C) Notepad
   (D) Clipboard

5. The taskbar displays _______.
   (A) All the programs currently open on your desktop
   (B) Programs currently open on your desktop and also display the programs which were closed in the previous session
   (C) Programs currently opened by you and all other users logged in to the system
   (D) All the programs installed on your computer

6. Full multitasking is not provided by which of the following operating systems?
   (A) Windows 8
   (B) Windows Vista
   (C) Windows XP
   (D) MS DOS

7. As soon as Windows starts up and you log in, you see the _______.
   (A) Icon   (B) Folder
   (C) Desktop   (D) Logo

8. When you shut down your Windows operating system computer, it automatically clears the contents of _________.
   (A) RAM
   (B) Hard Drive
   (C) Floppy Disk
   (D) None of these

9. You can display various toolbars on your taskbar by _______.
   (A) Right clicking on the Taskbar, then clicking Toolbars
   (B) Going to the Control Panel, Then clicking Toolbars
   (C) Right clicking on the Taskbar, then clicking Properties → Toolbars
   (D) All of these

10. Which of the following was not a version of Windows Vista?
    (A) Widows Vista Ultimate
    (B) Widows VistaStarter
    (C) Widows VistaOffice
    (D) Widows VistaBusiness

11. When Windows needs more information from you like confirmation to delete a file, the information is displayed in a _______.
    (A) Question box
    (B) Information box
    (C) Dialog box
    (D) Mail box

12. To save energy, a computer goes into the _______ mode for some time.
    (A) Sleep   (B) Shutdown
    (C) Slowdown   (D) Hibernate

13. _______ are links to programs, documents, files or websites that you can add to your desktop or Start menu.
    (A) .exe files   (B) Hyperlink
    (C) Shortcuts   (D) .bar files

14. Windows can run on _______.
    (A) 32-bit processors
    (B) 64-bit processors
    (C) 128 bit processors
    (D) Both (A) and (B)

15. A snapshot of desktop is given. Which version of Windows it is most likely from?

    (A) Windows 7
    (B) Windows 8
    (C) Windows XP
    (D) Windows Vista

16. Which of the following is not a version of Windows 7?
    (A) Windows 7 Ultimate
    (B) Windows 7 Professional
    (C) Windows 7 Maximum
    (D) Windows 7 Home Premium

17. The _______ in the Control Panel System Properties lists all the hardware devices installed on your computer.
    (A) Device Checker
    (B) Device Manager
    (C) Hardware Checker
    (D) Hardware Manager

18. _______ is a popular graphics program that is pre-installed on Windows 10. This program allows you to create, edit and print simple drawings and graphics.
    (A) Paint   (B) Paint Shop
    (C) Paint Brush   (D) Photo Shop

19. Identify the logo.

    (A) Windows Movie Maker
    (B) Windows Media Player

(C) Winamp7.2

(D) VLC Media Player

20. Identify the Windows start mode:
- In this mode, Windows starts with a limited set of files and drivers.
- This mode is useful for troubleshooting problems with programs and drivers.

- These programs or drivers might not start correctly.
- They may also prevent Windows from starting correctly.

(A) Safe mode

(B) Start mode

(C) Error free mode

(D) Troubleshoot mode

HOTS (ACHIEVERS SECTION)

21. In Windows operating system it is a window that is used to display text or to receive text from you. The type of text it displays or the type of text you are asked to provide depends on the application or the situation.

(A) Control's Focus

(B) Dialog Boxes

(C) Command Buttons

(D) Text Boxes

22. A __________ contains buttons and menus that provide quick access to commonly used commands.

(A) Toolbar   (B) Menu bar

(C) Window   (D) Find

23. The blinking symbol which indicates the next character will appear at which place, is called

(A) Delete key   (B) Control key

(C) Cursor   (D) Return key

24. Which of the following statements is false concerning file names?

(A) Files may share the same name or the same extension but not both.

(B) Every file in the same folder must have a unique name.

(C) File extension is another name for file type.

(D) None of these

25. The __________ settings are automatic and standard.

(A) Default

(B) CPU

(C) Peripheral

(D) User-friendly

1.	Ⓐ Ⓑ Ⓒ Ⓓ	6.	Ⓐ Ⓑ Ⓒ Ⓓ	11.	Ⓐ Ⓑ Ⓒ Ⓓ	16.	Ⓐ Ⓑ Ⓒ Ⓓ	21.	Ⓐ Ⓑ Ⓒ Ⓓ
2.	Ⓐ Ⓑ Ⓒ Ⓓ	7.	Ⓐ Ⓑ Ⓒ Ⓓ	12.	Ⓐ Ⓑ Ⓒ Ⓓ	17.	Ⓐ Ⓑ Ⓒ Ⓓ	22.	Ⓐ Ⓑ Ⓒ Ⓓ
3.	Ⓐ Ⓑ Ⓒ Ⓓ	8.	Ⓐ Ⓑ Ⓒ Ⓓ	13.	Ⓐ Ⓑ Ⓒ Ⓓ	18.	Ⓐ Ⓑ Ⓒ Ⓓ	23.	Ⓐ Ⓑ Ⓒ Ⓓ
4.	Ⓐ Ⓑ Ⓒ Ⓓ	9.	Ⓐ Ⓑ Ⓒ Ⓓ	14.	Ⓐ Ⓑ Ⓒ Ⓓ	19.	Ⓐ Ⓑ Ⓒ Ⓓ	24.	Ⓐ Ⓑ Ⓒ Ⓓ
5.	Ⓐ Ⓑ Ⓒ Ⓓ	10.	Ⓐ Ⓑ Ⓒ Ⓓ	15.	Ⓐ Ⓑ Ⓒ Ⓓ	20.	Ⓐ Ⓑ Ⓒ Ⓓ	25.	Ⓐ Ⓑ Ⓒ Ⓓ

MS WORD

LEARNING OBJECTIVES

➤ Ribbon in MS Word
➤ Numbering List

MULTIPLE CHOICE QUESTIONS

1. __________ is used to insert ghost text behind the content of the page. This text indicates that the document should be treated specially such as Sample, Urgent or Confidential.

   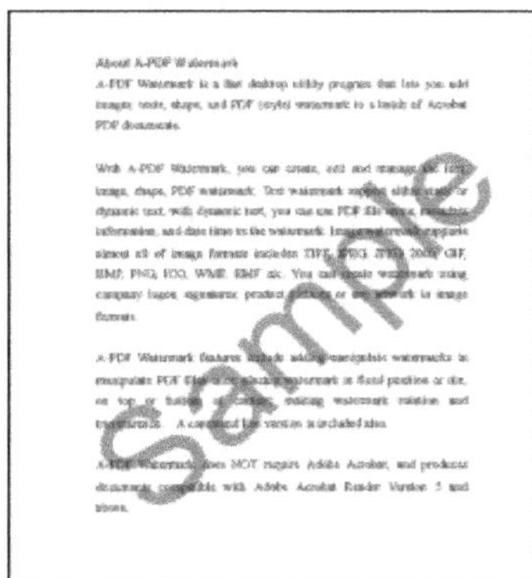

   (A) Background   (B) Watermark
   (C) Highlight   (D) Special

2. Match the following.

Column - I		Column - II
(i)	Font	(a)
(ii)	Font Style	(b)
(iii)	Font Size	(c) **B** *I* <u>U</u>
(iv)	Font Color	(d) Calibri

   (A) (i)-(c), (ii)-(a), (iii)-(b), (iv)-(d)
   (B) (i)-(d), (ii)-(a), (iii)-(c), (iv)-(b)
   (C) (i)-(d), (ii)-(c), (iii)-(b), (iv)-(a)
   (D) (i)-(d), (ii)-(c), (iii)-(a), (iv)-(b)

3. Identify the tool.
   - They are used to identify positions in a document.
   - These positions can be of a chapter or table.
   - It is also placed in a document where you left off.
   - They can be used to jump to specific points in documents.
   - You do not have to scroll or search through the page in the document.

   (A) Bookmarks   (B) Hyperlinks
   (C) Watermarks   (D) Save points

4. Which of the following is not valid in MS Word?
   (A) Print Layout   (B) Navigation
   (C) Outline   (D) Web Layout

5. `Ctrl` + `Shift` + `+ =` is used to format the text to __________.
   (A) Superscript
   (B) Subscript
   (C) Increase font size
   (D) Decrease font size

6. The Line numbers command is used to ________.
   (A) Add line numbers in the workspace along each side of the document
   (B) Add line number in the margin alongside of each line of the document
   (C) Show the paragraphs in the document
   (D) Show the line number where cursor is positioned

7. $Ctrl$ + $F2$ shortcut is used for ________.
   (A) Highlighting text
   (B) Scrolling text
   (C) Formatting text
   (D) Print preview

8. A ________ is a series of Word commands that you group together as a single operation to accomplish a task with a single click.
   (A) Macro
   (B) Automation
   (C) Execution
   (D) Statements

9. Identify the tool.
   - It refers to refreshing information.
   - This information can be headings, figures and tables in various parts of your document.
   - They are automatically updated if the content is moved to another location.
   (A) Cross-reference
   (B) Hyperlink
   (C) Direct reference
   (D) Link

10. Which of the following options shows the Strikethrough Effect?
    (A) ~~Strikethrough~~
    (B) ~~Strikethrough~~
    (C) ~~Strikethrough~~
    (D) ~~Strikethrough~~

11. The orientation of the following document is ________ orientation.

    (A) Portrait
    (B) Print
    (C) Table
    (D) Landscape

12. Which of the following is not available in Character Spacing?
    (A) Normal
    (B) Loosely
    (C) Condensed
    (D) Expanded

13. ![tool] tool is used to ________.
    (A) Clear all the formatting from the selection, leaving only the plain text
    (B) Clear all the formatting from the selection, leaving only the bold text
    (C) Clear all the formatting from the selection, leaving only the italic text
    (D) Delete all the selected text

14. Which feature automatically moves the text in the current line to the next line when such text does not fit on that line or when the page margins are altered?
    (A) Word Wrap   (B) Word Scroll
    (C) Word Format   (D) Word Enter

15. The highlight feature of Word highlights sections of text in up to ________ different colors.
    (A) 16   (B) 12
    (C) 14   (D) 15

16. In order to reach the end of the document, _______ key combination is pressed.

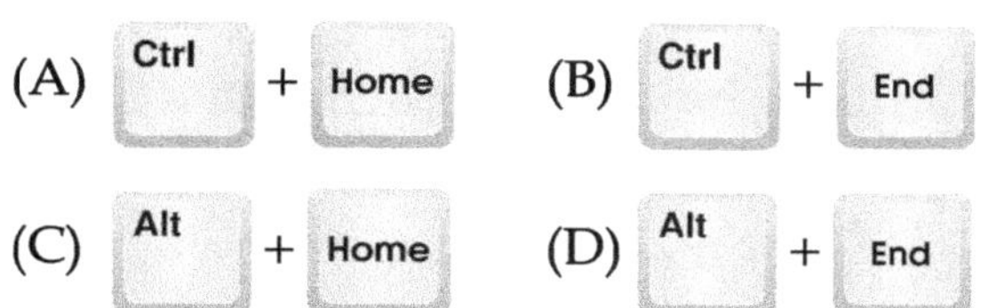

(A) Ctrl + Home   (B) Ctrl + End

(C) Alt + Home   (D) Alt + End

17. In order to change uppercase text to lowercase text and lowercase text to uppercase text, Change case > _______ is used.

(A) Title case

(B) Sentence case

(C) Lower case

(D) Toggle Case

18. In MS Word, you can set tabs by clicking on the _______.

(A) Horizontal Ruler

(B) Vertical Ruler

(C) Horizontal Scroll Bar

(D) Vertical Scroll Bar

19. To insert special characters like ©, ¥, ∞, click.

(A) View Tab > Special Characters

(B) View Tab –> Symbol

(C) Insert Tab –> Special Characters

(D) Insert Tab –> Symbol

20. _______ key combination is used to show paragraph marks and other hidden formatting symbols.

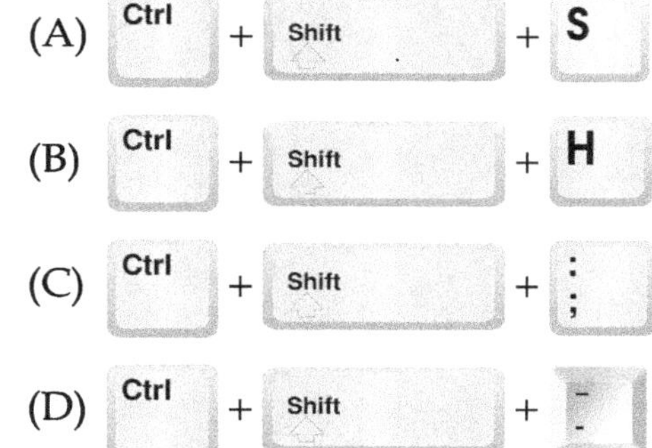

(A) Ctrl + Shift + S

(B) Ctrl + Shift + H

(C) Ctrl + Shift + ;

(D) Ctrl + Shift + -

HOTS (ACHIEVERS SECTION)

21. In MS Word, by switching to Print Layout view and then pressing Ctrl + Alt and the plus (+) sign on the numeric pad and press enter, the customize keyboard dialog box is displayed as shown in the figure. What does this command box display?

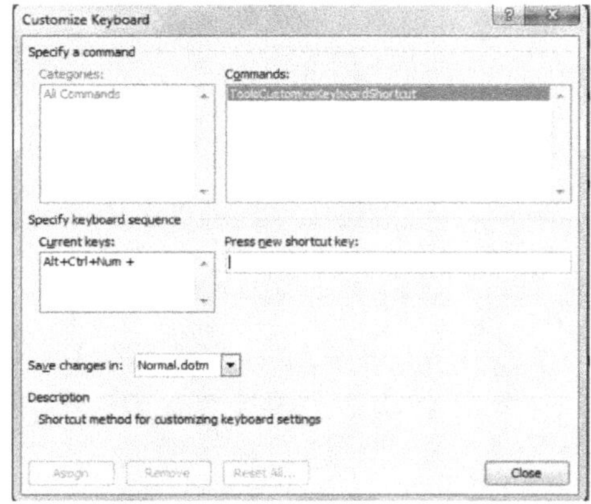

(A) Actual command's name

(B) Font size of the text

(C) Reveal text formatting

(D) Limited formatting to permitted styles

22. Background color or effects applied on a document is not visible in

(A) Web layout view

(B) Print Layout view

(C) Reading View

(D) Print Preview

23. Which of the following is used to create newspaper style columns?

(A) Format Columns

(B) Table Insert Table

(C) Insert Textbox

(D) Format Tabs

24. When typing in a word field manually, what must you press to insert the code's braces?

(A) Ctrl + F6
(B) Ctrl + F9
(C) Alt + F11
(D) Shift + F12

25. In MS Word, given window appears when the dialog box launcher in the Styles group of Home Tab is clicked. What are A, B and C here?

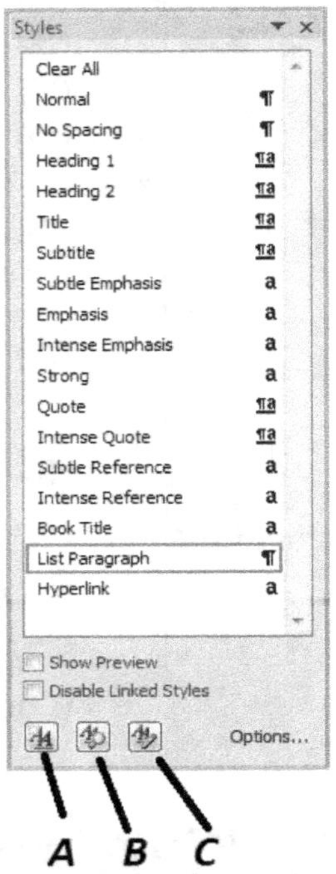

(A) A – New Style
   B – Manage Styles
   C – Style Inspector
(C) A – Style Inspector
   B – New Style
   C – Manage Styles

(B) A – New Style
   B – Style Inspector
   C – Manage Styles
(D) A – Manage Styles
   B – New Style
   C – Style Inspector

1.	Ⓐ Ⓑ Ⓒ Ⓓ	6.	Ⓐ Ⓑ Ⓒ Ⓓ	11.	Ⓐ Ⓑ Ⓒ Ⓓ	16.	Ⓐ Ⓑ Ⓒ Ⓓ	21.	Ⓐ Ⓑ Ⓒ Ⓓ
2.	Ⓐ Ⓑ Ⓒ Ⓓ	7.	Ⓐ Ⓑ Ⓒ Ⓓ	12.	Ⓐ Ⓑ Ⓒ Ⓓ	17.	Ⓐ Ⓑ Ⓒ Ⓓ	22.	Ⓐ Ⓑ Ⓒ Ⓓ
3.	Ⓐ Ⓑ Ⓒ Ⓓ	8.	Ⓐ Ⓑ Ⓒ Ⓓ	13.	Ⓐ Ⓑ Ⓒ Ⓓ	18.	Ⓐ Ⓑ Ⓒ Ⓓ	23.	Ⓐ Ⓑ Ⓒ Ⓓ
4.	Ⓐ Ⓑ Ⓒ Ⓓ	9.	Ⓐ Ⓑ Ⓒ Ⓓ	14.	Ⓐ Ⓑ Ⓒ Ⓓ	19.	Ⓐ Ⓑ Ⓒ Ⓓ	24.	Ⓐ Ⓑ Ⓒ Ⓓ
5.	Ⓐ Ⓑ Ⓒ Ⓓ	10.	Ⓐ Ⓑ Ⓒ Ⓓ	15.	Ⓐ Ⓑ Ⓒ Ⓓ	20.	Ⓐ Ⓑ Ⓒ Ⓓ	25.	Ⓐ Ⓑ Ⓒ Ⓓ

MS POWERPOINT

MULTIPLE CHOICE QUESTIONS

1. Which of the following font styles is not available in the PowerPoint Font dialog box?
   (A) Double Strike through
   (B) Small Caps
   (C) Emboss
   (D) Strike through

2. What is an object in PowerPoint?
   (A) Anything that gets inserted and not used in a finished presentation.
   (B) The thing you are aiming to do with your complete presentation
   (C) The term used to do with your completed presentation
   (D) Anything put in a slide such as clip art, sound effects, images

3. To customize the ribbon, you must _____.
   (A) Use the "Customized Quick Access Toolbar" to the "Customize the Ribbon".
   (B) Right click on the PowerPoint Menu Bar, then click on the "Customize the Ribbon".
   (C) Left click on the Ribbon and then click on the "Customized the Ribbon".
   (D) Right click on the Ribbon, then click on the "Customize the Ribbon.

4. Which of the following statements is true?
   (A) You can insert text boxes from the Insert Tab of the ribbon.
   (B) You can insert text boxes from the Design Tab of the ribbon.
   (C) Text boxes are provided when you select a layout. They cannot be inserted after you have selected a layout.
   (D) None of these.

5. The _____ command is used to show or hide the ribbon.
   (A) Ctrl + F2   (B) Ctrl + F1
   (C) Ctrl + F3   (D) Alt + F1

6. Which option would you select from the print options to print slides 5 and 12 of a presentation?
   (A) Slides
   (B) Full Page Slides
   (C) Collated
   (D) All sides

7. Which of the following is not an option for printing handouts?
   (A) Six slides per page
   (B) Five slides per page
   (C) Three slides per page
   (D) Two slides per page

8. Press _________ or go to _________ to insert the 'New Slides'.

(A) **Ctrl** + **M** , Home → New Slide

(B) **Ctrl** + **M** , File → New Slide

(C) **Ctrl** + **M** , Insert → New Slide

(D) **Ctrl** + **M** , File → New Slide

9. Predefined designs called _________ regulate the formatting and layout for the PowerPoint slide.
   (A) Design Plates   (B) Templates
   (C) Placeholders   (D) Blueprints

10. Header and Footer are by default present in _________ view.
    (A) Tile master
    (B) Slide Master
    (C) Handout Master
    (D) Page Master

11. What is the optimal method to create slide layouts?
    (A) Using the Master Layout dialog box in the slide master view
    (B) Select the layout from the slide layout popup
    (C) Use slide design templates
    (D) None of these

12. To go to the backstage view, click the _________.
    (A) Power Point Application Button
    (B) Home Tab
    (C) File Tab
    (D) View Tab

13. You use the Microsoft clip gallery to _________.
    (A) Add Word Art image to slides
    (B) Spell check in a presentation
    (C) Add clip art images to slides
    (D) Add new slides to graphics to a presentation

14. The option shown by dropdown below is used to _________.

(A) Display the Slide Sorter view
(B) To Play the Slide show
(C) Display the Reading view
(D) Fit Slide to Current window

15. Separating a clipart into different parts such that each part becomes a different object is called _________.
    (A) Separation   (B) Regrouping
    (C) Ungrouping   (D) Unmerging

16. Special effects can be applied to various drawing objects. Which of the following shows gradient pattern?
    (A) Shape Fill   (B) Shape Outline
    (C) Shape Effects   (D) All of these

17. Identify the icon shown here.

(A) Layout   (B) Reset
(C) Section   (D) New Slide

18. While resizing, to maintain the height and width ratio of an object, you must _________.
    (A) Press and hold the **Shift** key while dragging a corner size handle.
    (B) Press and hold the **Alt** + **Ctrl** keys while dragging a middle handle.

(C) Drag a corner size handle.
(D) All of these

19. Animation scheme can be applied to ______ in the presentation.
(A) All slides
(B) Selected slides
(C) Current slides
(D) All of these

20. While an image is selected, it displays ______ corner handles.
(A) Two
(B) Four
(C) Six
(D) Eight

HOTS (ACHIEVERS SECTION)

21. An image of Animation Pane in MS PowerPoint is shown here. What does number (A) represent?

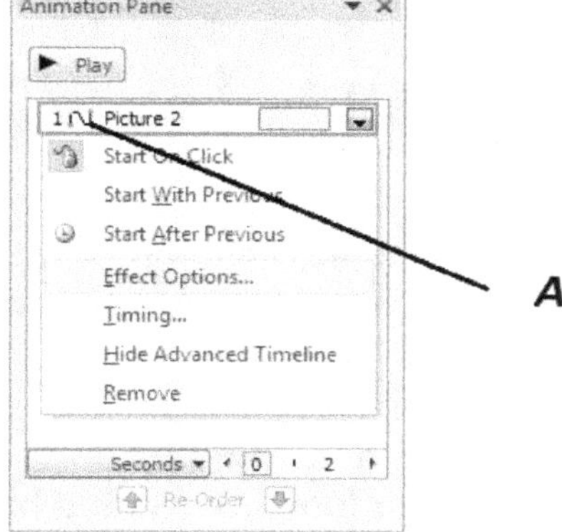

(A) Indicates more events are collapsed
(B) Means animation will occur on click
(C) Indicates entrance effect
(D) Indicates mouse click

22. It is the default setting for manual text boxes in MS-PowerPoint. Which of the following text boxes auto fit behaviour enlarges the text box to the size needed to contain the text?
(A) Do Not AutoFit
(B) Shrink Text on Overflow
(C) Resize Shape to Fit Text
(D) All of these

23. Which of the following provides a means of printing out feature notes with a miniature slide on a printed page?
(A) Slide with animation
(B) Outline view
(C) Notes page
(D) Audience handout

24. The PowerPoint view that displays only text (title and bullets) is
(A) Slide show
(B) Slide sorter view
(C) Notes page view
(D) Outline view

25. Objects on the slide that hold text are called
(A) Placeholders
(B) Object holders
(C) Auto layout
(D) Text holders

--------Darken Your Choice with HB Pencil--------

	A	B	C	D			A	B	C	D			A	B	C	D			A	B	C	D			A	B	C	D
1.	Ⓐ	Ⓑ	Ⓒ	Ⓓ	6.	Ⓐ	Ⓑ	Ⓒ	Ⓓ	11.	Ⓐ	Ⓑ	Ⓒ	Ⓓ	16.	Ⓐ	Ⓑ	Ⓒ	Ⓓ	21.	Ⓐ	Ⓑ	Ⓒ	Ⓓ
2.	Ⓐ	Ⓑ	Ⓒ	Ⓓ	7.	Ⓐ	Ⓑ	Ⓒ	Ⓓ	12.	Ⓐ	Ⓑ	Ⓒ	Ⓓ	17.	Ⓐ	Ⓑ	Ⓒ	Ⓓ	22.	Ⓐ	Ⓑ	Ⓒ	Ⓓ
3.	Ⓐ	Ⓑ	Ⓒ	Ⓓ	8.	Ⓐ	Ⓑ	Ⓒ	Ⓓ	13.	Ⓐ	Ⓑ	Ⓒ	Ⓓ	18.	Ⓐ	Ⓑ	Ⓒ	Ⓓ	23.	Ⓐ	Ⓑ	Ⓒ	Ⓓ
4.	Ⓐ	Ⓑ	Ⓒ	Ⓓ	9.	Ⓐ	Ⓑ	Ⓒ	Ⓓ	14.	Ⓐ	Ⓑ	Ⓒ	Ⓓ	19.	Ⓐ	Ⓑ	Ⓒ	Ⓓ	24.	Ⓐ	Ⓑ	Ⓒ	Ⓓ
5.	Ⓐ	Ⓑ	Ⓒ	Ⓓ	10.	Ⓐ	Ⓑ	Ⓒ	Ⓓ	15.	Ⓐ	Ⓑ	Ⓒ	Ⓓ	20.	Ⓐ	Ⓑ	Ⓒ	Ⓓ	25.	Ⓐ	Ⓑ	Ⓒ	Ⓓ

INTRODUCTION TO QBASIC

LEARNING OBJECTIVES

➤ Basics of QBasic

MULTIPLE CHOICE QUESTIONS

1. In QBASIC, description comments are put in the source program with the _______ statement.
   (A) PRINT
   (B) INPUT
   (C) REMARK
   (D) DATA

2. Which of these is a valid numeric variable name?
   (A) M8
   (B) 8M
   (C) $M
   (D) 2B43

3. Numeric constants (integer type) refer to numbers in the range _______ to _______.
   (A) – 32786, + 32786
   (B) – 32768, + 32768
   (C) – 32755, + 32755
   (D) – 32789, + 32785

4. LET is called _______ statement.
   (A) Input
   (B) Output
   (C) Loop
   (D) Assignment

5. What will treat the rest of the line as a comment?
   (A) REM
   (B) Apostrophe

   (C) Both (A) and (B)
   (D) None of these

6. Which of the following statements is true for a Nested loop?
   (A) A loop that begins first and ends last.
   (B) A loop that begins first and ends last.
   (C) The outer loop is executed before the inner loop.
   (D) None of these

7. REM stands for _______.
   (A) Remark
   (B) Remove
   (C) Remain
   (D) Remote

8. Which command do you use to delete an item on the hard drive?
   (A) KILL
   (B) DEL
   (C) DELETE
   (D) CLS

9. Which of the following statements is not true for variable?
   (A) Variable name can begin with letter of the English alphabet.
   (B) Variable name can begin with a special character.
   (C) Variable name cannot be a reserved word.

(D) Alphanumeric variable names must end with a $ sign.

10. Which command is used for clear output screen?
    (A) CLS
    (B) CLEAR
    (C) RUB
    (D) ERASE

11. Which of the following statements is true for the GO TO statement?
    (A) Instruct the computer to go to a specific line number
    (B) It can be used to skip some statements.
    (C) It can be used to repeat some statements.
    (D) All of these

12. ______ sets the position where the next character will be shown on the screen or printed on paper.
    (A) TAB
    (B) INPUT
    (C) WRITE
    (D) PRINT

13. BASIC is a programming language developed at ________College in 1964.
    (A) MIT
    (B) Dartmouth
    (C) Wayne
    (D) Sequenced

14. A loop within a loop is called _____ loop.
    (A) Combined
    (B) Nested
    (C) Jumbled
    (D) Sequenced

15. ______ statement is used to stop and get information from a user using a question mark.
    (A) INPUT
    (B) GET
    (C) QUERY
    (D) QUESTION

16. Given below is a QBASIC program which is not printing any value. Find the error in the given QBASIC program:
    ```
    10 PRINT "Enter a number, zero to stop:;
    20 input A
    30 IF A THEN GO TO 70
    40 LET A = A + 10
    50 PRINT "The number plus 10 is", A
    60 GO TO 10
    70 STOP
    ```
    (A) The error is on the line 10.
    (B) The error is on the line 30.
    (C) The error is on the line 50.
    (D) There are no errors.

17. You can run the program by pressing ______.
    (A) F2
    (B) CTRL + ALT + DEL
    (C) Shift + F5
    (D) Double right click

18. Name$ is a ______.
    (A) Numerical constant
    (B) Numerical Variable
    (C) String Constant
    (D) String Variable

19. Which of the following is NOT a QBASIC operator?
    (A) < =
    (B) > =
    (C) < >
    (D) – >

20. What value will be printed after the successful execution of the following codes?
    ```
    LET C = 0
    DO WHILE C < 10
    LET C = C + 1
    LOOP
    PRINT C
    ```
    (A) 0
    (B) 1
    (C) 10
    (D) 11

21. What does SOUND command in QBASIC actually do?
    (A) It produces a beep sound that lasts for about half a second.
    (B) It produces sound of a specific frequency for a specific duration from the PC speaker.
    (C) It is used to set the screen attribute.
    (D) It is used to display pixels on screen.

22. Find the output of the given QBASIC code.

    A$ = "Hello" + "WORLD"

    PRINT A$

    (A) HelloWORLD
    (B) Hello + WORLD
    (C) Helloworld
    (D) "Hello" + "WORLD"

23. How do you draw pixels in QBasic?
    (A) PSET   (B) DRAW
    (C) PXL   (D) DRWPX

24. Which version of QBasic can make programs into .EXE files?
    (A) QB 8.4   (B) QB 1.1
    (C) QB 4.5   (D) QB 3.2

25. What will be the output of the following code?

    10 REM EXAMPLE OF HOW A COMMA
    20 REM AFFECTS THE OUTPUT
    30 REM PRINT STATEMENT
    40 PRINT "4 + 7 =",
    50 PRINT 4 + 7
    60 PRINT END

    (A) 4 + 7   (B) 4 + 7 = 11
    (C) 11   (D) All of these

Darken Your Choice with HB Pencil

	A	B	C	D			A	B	C	D			A	B	C	D			A	B	C	D			A	B	C	D
1.	Ⓐ	Ⓑ	Ⓒ	Ⓓ	6.	Ⓐ	Ⓑ	Ⓒ	Ⓓ	11.	Ⓐ	Ⓑ	Ⓒ	Ⓓ	16.	Ⓐ	Ⓑ	Ⓒ	Ⓓ	21.	Ⓐ	Ⓑ	Ⓒ	Ⓓ
2.	Ⓐ	Ⓑ	Ⓒ	Ⓓ	7.	Ⓐ	Ⓑ	Ⓒ	Ⓓ	12.	Ⓐ	Ⓑ	Ⓒ	Ⓓ	17.	Ⓐ	Ⓑ	Ⓒ	Ⓓ	22.	Ⓐ	Ⓑ	Ⓒ	Ⓓ
3.	Ⓐ	Ⓑ	Ⓒ	Ⓓ	8.	Ⓐ	Ⓑ	Ⓒ	Ⓓ	13.	Ⓐ	Ⓑ	Ⓒ	Ⓓ	18.	Ⓐ	Ⓑ	Ⓒ	Ⓓ	23.	Ⓐ	Ⓑ	Ⓒ	Ⓓ
4.	Ⓐ	Ⓑ	Ⓒ	Ⓓ	9.	Ⓐ	Ⓑ	Ⓒ	Ⓓ	14.	Ⓐ	Ⓑ	Ⓒ	Ⓓ	19.	Ⓐ	Ⓑ	Ⓒ	Ⓓ	24.	Ⓐ	Ⓑ	Ⓒ	Ⓓ
5.	Ⓐ	Ⓑ	Ⓒ	Ⓓ	10.	Ⓐ	Ⓑ	Ⓒ	Ⓓ	15.	Ⓐ	Ⓑ	Ⓒ	Ⓓ	20.	Ⓐ	Ⓑ	Ⓒ	Ⓓ	25.	Ⓐ	Ⓑ	Ⓒ	Ⓓ

INTERNET AND E-MAIL

LEARNING OBJECTIVES

➤ Fundamentals of Internet
➤ Internet Explorer
➤ Email

MULTIPLE CHOICE QUESTIONS

1. __________ are the networks that connect departments within a school to each other and the school network also.
   (A) School networks (B) Intranets
   (C) Extranets (D) Internets

2. When your organization is using networks like intranets and Internet to conduct business, it is conducting _____.
   (A) E-procurement (B) E-business
   (C) E-commerce (D) E-marketing

3. Which of the following is not used to connect to the Internet?
   (A) ISDN (B) DSL
   (C) VDU (D) MODEM

4. You use a ______ to find information on the Internet.
   (A) Admin Point
   (B) Search Portal
   (C) Information Kiosk
   (D) Access point

5. The temporary storage area that the IE uses to store graphics and web pages which have been recently viewed, is called ______.
   (A) Cache (B) RAM
   (C) RO (D) Flash

6. A website which can be viewed by anybody in the world, is generally hosted on a ______.
   (A) Page server
   (B) Data server
   (C) Web Server
   (D) Information server

7. When talking about networking and Internet, what is a port?
   (A) An external output device.
   (B) An input device.
   (C) It's the protocol e-mail messages have to follow to travel over the Internet.
   (D) It's a data connection that allows information transfer to and from a specific server process.

8. This WordArt ~~contribute~~ is commonly seen during verification. This is known as ______.
   (A) Crypt (B) Word art
   (C) Code (D) Captcha

9. The ______ method of access requires a user to be connected to the Internet through an ordinary telephone line.
   (A) Dedicated access
   (B) Dial up access

(C) FTP

(D) None of these

10. Safari is a ______.
    (A) Web browser
    (B) New reader
    (C) Graphing package
    (D) None of these

11. AltaVista and Hotbot are examples of ______.

    (A) Web games
    (B) Social networks
    (C) Search engines
    (D) Stand–alone program

12. Some web applications maintain the list of websites and a brief summary of their content in large databases. These large databases are called ______ and these web applications are called ______.
    (A) Search Engines, Indexes
    (B) Indexes, Search Engines
    (C) Hyperlink, WebPages
    (D) None of these

13. Internet Explorer was developed by ______.

    (A) Sun microsystems

    (B) Microsoft

    (C) (Apple)

    (D) ORACLE

14. Web addresses can be written as words or as numbers. What are these numbers/words called?

    For example, www.mywebsite.org might have address number of 63.141.53.0
    (A) Uniform Resource Locator number
    (B) Internet Protocol address
    (C) File Transfer Protocol address
    (D) Web addresses can only be accessed by names.

15. If you receive an e-mail with an attachment from a company saying you just won a video game system, but you have not ever heard of the person who has sent the e-mail, what should you do?
    (A) Go to the website and fill in the information to get your prize.
    (B) Delete the e-mail.
    (C) Delete the attachment only.
    (D) Contact the person who sent you the e-mail.

16. Several Internet programs systematically browse the internet. They mainly and periodically do such systematic browsing for web indexing. This process of indexing is also known as______.
    (A) Filtering   (B) Crawling
    (C) Phishing   (D) None of these

17. Match the following.

	Column - I		Column - II
(i)	Negatives Search	(a)	'+"
(ii)	Common words can be made essential in search by	(b)	"I'm feeling lucky"
(iii)	Phrase search	(c)	"–"
(iv)	Opens the first and most relevant website	(d)	" "

    (A) (i)–(c), (ii)–(b), (iii)–(c), (iv)–(a)
    (B) (i)–(c), (ii)–(a), (iii)–(d), (iv)–(b)
    (C) (i)–(b), (ii)–(c), (iii)–(d), (iv)–(a)
    (D) (i)–(b), (ii)–(c), (iii)–(a), (iv)–(d)

18. In the web address,
    http//:www.myhomepage.com/pictures/myschool/classvi.jpg
    What does myschool indicate?
    (A) The name of the image on the website.
    (B) It is the URL.
    (C) The folder where ClassVI.JPG is found.
    (D) The homepage image for the website www.myhomepage.com.

19. A snapshot of Google chrome is given here. What is the encircled bar shown here called?

(A) Menu bar   (B) Task bar
(C) Address bar   (D) Current bar

20. Which of them is/was not a social networking site?

(A) orkut

(B) myspace

(C) altavista

(D) facebook

HOTS (ACHIEVERS SECTION)

21. Select the INCORRECT match.
    (A) www.ixquic.com – Search engine
    (B) Filehippo.com – provide technology news and reviews
    (C) Amazon.com – Online shopping site
    (D) Both (A) and (B)

22. Which of the following statements is correct?
    (A) File server provides a central storage facility to store files of several users on a network.
    (B) The server translates name into network addresses.
    (C) Database server manages a centralized database and enables several users on a network to have shared access to same database.
    (D) All of these

23. Suppose, a webpage owner updated his webpage, then which of the following would find those changes and update its index?
    (A) HotBot   (B) Spider
    (C) Lycos   (D) Inference find

24. What is the only restriction that computers have while messaging via e-mail?
    (A) Data should not be in .rtf format.
    (B) Data should not be in .odt format.
    (C) Data should not be in .docx format.
    (D) Data should be in readable format.

25. _____are attempt by individuals to obtain confidential information from you by falsifying their identity:
    (A) Phishing Trips
    (B) Computer Viruses
    (C) Spyware Scams
    (D) Viruses

Darken Your Choice with HB Pencil

1.	Ⓐ Ⓑ Ⓒ Ⓓ	6.	Ⓐ Ⓑ Ⓒ Ⓓ	11.	Ⓐ Ⓑ Ⓒ Ⓓ	16.	Ⓐ Ⓑ Ⓒ Ⓓ	21.	Ⓐ Ⓑ Ⓒ Ⓓ
2.	Ⓐ Ⓑ Ⓒ Ⓓ	7.	Ⓐ Ⓑ Ⓒ Ⓓ	12.	Ⓐ Ⓑ Ⓒ Ⓓ	17.	Ⓐ Ⓑ Ⓒ Ⓓ	22.	Ⓐ Ⓑ Ⓒ Ⓓ
3.	Ⓐ Ⓑ Ⓒ Ⓓ	8.	Ⓐ Ⓑ Ⓒ Ⓓ	13.	Ⓐ Ⓑ Ⓒ Ⓓ	18.	Ⓐ Ⓑ Ⓒ Ⓓ	23.	Ⓐ Ⓑ Ⓒ Ⓓ
4.	Ⓐ Ⓑ Ⓒ Ⓓ	9.	Ⓐ Ⓑ Ⓒ Ⓓ	14.	Ⓐ Ⓑ Ⓒ Ⓓ	19.	Ⓐ Ⓑ Ⓒ Ⓓ	24.	Ⓐ Ⓑ Ⓒ Ⓓ
5.	Ⓐ Ⓑ Ⓒ Ⓓ	10.	Ⓐ Ⓑ Ⓒ Ⓓ	15.	Ⓐ Ⓑ Ⓒ Ⓓ	20.	Ⓐ Ⓑ Ⓒ Ⓓ	25.	Ⓐ Ⓑ Ⓒ Ⓓ

LATEST DEVELOPMENTS IN 'IT' 

9

- ➤ Internet of Things
- ➤ Machine Learning
- ➤ Virtual Reality

MULTIPLE CHOICE QUESTIONS

1. OLED stands for ______.
   - (A) Output Light Emitting Diode
   - (B) Organic Light Emitting Diode
   - (C) Organic Light Emitted Diode
   - (D) Organic Light Emitting Dioded

2. The image shown here is a ______.
   - (A) PDA
   - (B) Smartphone
   - (C) Notepad
   - (D) Convertible Laptop

3. Which of the following is incorrect about Apple 4th Generation Watch?
   - (A) It was revealed during the 2018 Apple Special Event held at the Steve Jobs Theater in California.
   - (B) It runs on Windows Platform.
   - (C) It features larger displays with thinner bezels and rounded corners, a slightly rounder, thinner chassis with a redesigned ceramic back
   - (D) It can also detect falls and will automatically contact emergency services unless the user cancels the outgoing call.

4. ______ is a software for iPhone from Apple that provides users with personal assistant which can perform various tasks based on the user's voice commands.
   - (A) Pulse
   - (B) Dragon
   - (C) Siri
   - (D) Safari

5. ______ is not an iPhone 8 feature.
   - (A) 5.8 inch OLED display
   - (B) Front fingerprint sensor
   - (C) Single Sim
   - (D) 12 MP Rear camera

6. Identify logo of ______.

   - (A) Bosch
   - (B) Infrared
   - (C) Wi-Fi
   - (D) Whatsapp

7. The digital payment system from Google is known as ______.
   - (A) Google Payment
   - (B) Google Pay
   - (C) Google Money
   - (D) Google Cheques

8. ______ is an information visualization software for animation of statistics that was initially developed by Hans Rosling's Gapminder Foundation in

Sweden. In March 2007 it was acquired by Google.

(A) FB Chat

(B) FB Skype

(C) Google + Face Tim

(D) Trendalyzer

9. Microsoft's personal cloud storage service is called _______.

(A) One Note   (B) SoftDocs

(C) MicroDocs   (D) One Drive

10. _________ is a web-based version of Microsoft's office suite of enterprise-grade applications.

(A) Microsoft Office 2013

(B) Libre Office

(C) Office 365

(D) Microsoft Back Office

11. What version of the Corel Draw Graphics suite was released on 12th March 2019 called?

(A) Corel Draw X9

(B) Corel DRAW Graphics Suit 2019

(C) Corel DRAW X6

(D) Corel DRAW X8

12. _______ is internet marketing formula used to calculate and quote the price on online advertisements.

(A) Pay per impression

(B) Pay per view

(C) Pay per use

(D) Pay per click

13. Which of the following statements is not true for Search Engine Optimization?

(A) A methodology of strategies, techniques and tactics.

(B) It works by obtaining a high-ranking placement in the search results page of a search engine.

(C) It is mainly run by Google.

(D) It is used to increase the amount of visitors to a website.

14. Who has been appointed as the new CEO of Microsoft on Feb 4, 2014?

(A) Satya Nadella

(B) Anshu Jain

(C) Indra

(D) Nooyi

15. Which of the following is true about iPad Air?

(A) It offers 64-bit Apple A7 processor.

(B) It uses MIMO technology.

(C) It was released on November 1, 2013.

(D) All of these.

16. In Windows 8, the Start Menu is replaced by _________.

(A) Start Tab

(B) Start Bar

(C) Start Notification

(D) Start Screen

17. In Windows 8, the screen that is displayed before the log-in screen is known as the _______. It can be used to show your next appointment or important notifications.

(A) Charms Screen

(B) Command Screen

(C) Lock Screen

(D) Running Apps Screen

18. The latest version of Xbox is _______.

(A) Xbox 777   (B) Xbox One

(C) Xbox Series X   (D) Xbox Live

19. Which of the following statements is not correct about the Mailbox app?

(A) It is a free e-mail management application for IOS.

(B) It does not work with Gmail.

(C) It was released in 2013.

(D) It is developed by Orchestra, Inc.

20. Google News is an aggregator. It watches more than _______ sources to get news.

(A) 1000   (B) 2500

(C) 4500   (D) 10000

21. Which of the following statements is correct about the given logo?

    snapdragon™

    (A) It is a family of mobile systems on a chip by Qualcomm.
    (B) It is the latest video game.
    (C) It is an I/O interface.
    (D) It is an app developed by Apple Inc.

22. HTC one Max is an Android Phablet smartphone developed by HTC. It runs on the Android 4.3 JellyBean with ______ operating system.
    (A) Sense 4.3
    (B) Sense 7.8
    (C) Sense 9.1
    (D) Sense 5.5

23. ______ is a high-end 4G touch screen, smartphone developed by Black Berry and it was released on September 18, 2013.
    (A) BlackBerry Z10   (B) BlackBerry Z30
    (C) BlackBerry Z20   (D) BlackBerry 230

24. NASA astronaut Kate Rubins has for the first-time harvested ______ crop at the International Space Station in Nov 2020.
    (A) Soybean   (B) Radish
    (C) Cotton   (D) Carrot

25. Which of the following is the deep sea search vehicle used to locate the missing Malaysian MH 370 flight?
    (A) Phoenix-NV   (B) Bluefin-21
    (C) Nereus-AUV   (D) Remus 6000

Darken Your Choice with HB Pencil

1.	A B C D	6.	A B C D	11.	A B C D	16.	A B C D	21.	A B C D
2.	A B C D	7.	A B C D	12.	A B C D	17.	A B C D	22.	A B C D
3.	A B C D	8.	A B C D	13.	A B C D	18.	A B C D	23.	A B C D
4.	A B C D	9.	A B C D	14.	A B C D	19.	A B C D	24.	A B C D
5.	A B C D	10.	A B C D	15.	A B C D	20.	A B C D	25.	A B C D

LOGICAL REASONING

LEARNING OBJECTIVES

- ➤ Analogy
- ➤ Concept of Odd One Out
- ➤ Alphabet Test
- ➤ Blood Relations
- ➤ Direction Sense Test
- ➤ Different type of Seating Arrangement
- ➤ Syllogism
- ➤ Venn Diagram
- ➤ Mirror Images of Numbers & Letters
- ➤ Water Images
- ➤ Embedded Figures
- ➤ Figure Matrix

MULTIPLE CHOICE QUESTIONS

Choose the correct option to replace the question mark.

1. Doctor : Patient :: ? : Employer:
   - (A) Employee
   - (B) Leader
   - (C) Worker
   - (D) Manager

2. Moon : Earth :: Thebe : ?
   - (A) Sun
   - (B) Planet
   - (C) Jupiter
   - (D) Asteroid

3. Bread : Butter : : Rajma : ?
   - (A) Chapati
   - (B) Daal
   - (C) Chawal
   - (D) Ghee

4. Find the odd one out.
   - (A) Mars
   - (B) Pluto
   - (C) Earth
   - (D) Saturn

5. Find the odd one out.
   - (A) Cricket
   - (B) Hockey
   - (C) Swimming
   - (D) Volley ball

6. Find the odd one out.
   - (A) Wheat
   - (B) Maize
   - (C) Rice
   - (D) Pea

Directions (1–10): In the following letter series, some letters are missing. Choose the correct alternative to fill in the blanks.

7. _ op _ mo _ n _ _ pnmop _.
   - (A) mnpmon
   - (B) mpnmop
   - (C) mnompn
   - (D) mnpomn

8. _bcc _ ac _ aabb _ ab _ cc
   - (A) aabca
   - (B) abaca
   - (C) bacab
   - (D) bcaca

9. m _ nm _ n _ an _ a _ ma _
    (A) aamnan
    (B) ammanm
    (C) aammnn
    (D) amammn

10. Pointing to a man on the stage, Ritu said, "He is the brother of the daughter of the wife of my husband." How is the man on the stage related to Ritu?
    (A) Husband
    (B) Cousin
    (C) Nephew
    (D) Son

11. A party consists of grandmother, father, mother, four sons and their wives and one son and two daughters to each of the sons. How many females are there in all?
    (A) 14
    (B) 19
    (C) 12
    (D) 25

12. Lata and Mona are Ravi's wives. Shalu is Mona's Step-daughter. How is Lata related to Shalu?
    (A) Sister
    (B) Mother-in-Law
    (C) Mother
    (D) Step-mother

13. A man is facing west. He turns 45 degree in the clockwise direction and then another 180 degree in the same direction and then 90 degree in the clockwise direction. Which direction is he facing now?
    (A) North
    (B) West
    (D) South
    (D) East-South

14. One day, Ravi cycled 20 Km southwards, turned right and cycled 10 Km and turned right and cycled 20 Km and turned left and cycled 10 Km. How many kilometres will he have to cycle to reach his home straight?
    (A) 50 Km
    (B) 20 Km
    (C) 40 Km
    (D) 30 Km

15. Vicky walked 10 Km towards North. From there, he walks 6 Km towards South. Then, he walks 2 Km towards West. How far and in which direction is he with reference to his starting point?
    (A) 5 Km, North
    (B) 6 Km, South
    (C) 5 Km, East
    (D) 6 Km, North-west

Directions (1–6): Read the information given in the questions and on the basis of the information, select the correct option.

(i) P, Q, R, S, T, U, and V, W are sitting in a circle facing the center.

(ii) P sits second to the right of W who is 3rd to the left of T.

(iii) S and T are immediate neighbours of R and V.

(iv) V sits between R and S.

(v) V is not an immediate neighbour to T.

16. Who is next to S?
    (A) P
    (B) Q
    (C) R
    (D) V

17. Who is second to the left of V?
    (A) U
    (B) Q
    (C) R
    (D) T

18. Who is immediate right of P?
    (A) Q   (B) T
    (C) S   (D) U

OLYMPIAD WORKBOOK (NCO) CLASS – 6

19. **Statements:** Some chairs are tables. All the tables are desks.

Conclusions:
1. All the tables are chairs.
2. Some chairs are desks.

(A) Only (1) conclusion follows
(B) Only (2) conclusion follows
(C) Either (1) or (2) follows
(D) Neither (1) nor (2) follows

20. **Statements:** Some bottles are plates. All the spoons are plates.

Conclusions:
1. Some plates are spoons.
2. Some plates are bottles.

(A) Only (1) conclusion follows
(B) Only (2) conclusion follows
(C) Either (1) or (2) follows
(D) Both (1) and (2) follow

21. **Statements:** All the guitars are instruments. All the instruments are harps.

Conclusions:
1. All the harps are instruments.
2. All the guitars are harps.

(A) Only (1) conclusion follows
(B) Only (2) conclusion follows
(C) Either (1) or (2) follows
(D) Neither (1) nor (2) follows

22. Choose the correct mirror image of the given numerals from amongst the four alternatives.

247596

(A) 695742
(B) 247596 [mirror]
(C) 695742 [mirror]
(D) 247596 [mirror]

23. Choose the correct mirror image of the given word from amongst the four alternatives.

GEOGRAPHY

(A) GEOGRAPHY [mirror]
(B) YHPARGOEG
(C) GEOGRAPHY [mirror]
(D) YHPARGOEG [mirror]

24. Choose the correct mirror image of the given word from amongst the four alternatives.

PAINTED

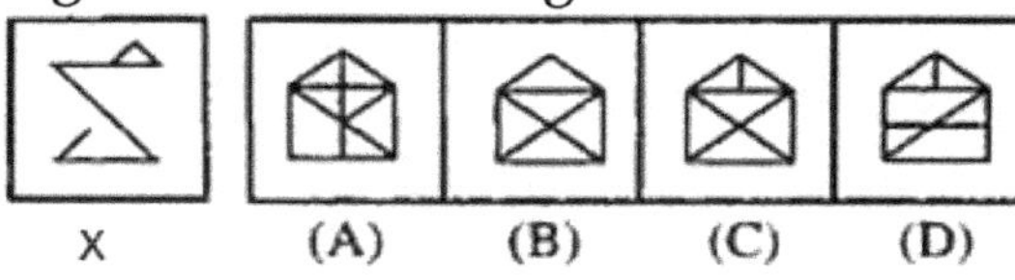

(A) PAINTED [mirror]
(B) PAINTED [mirror]
(C) PAINTED [mirror]
(D) PAINTED [mirror]

25. Find out the alternative figure which contains figure (X) as its part.

Figure   Answer Figures

(A) A
(B) B
(C) C
(D) D

26. Find out the alternative figure which contains figure (X) as its part.

Figure   Answer Figures

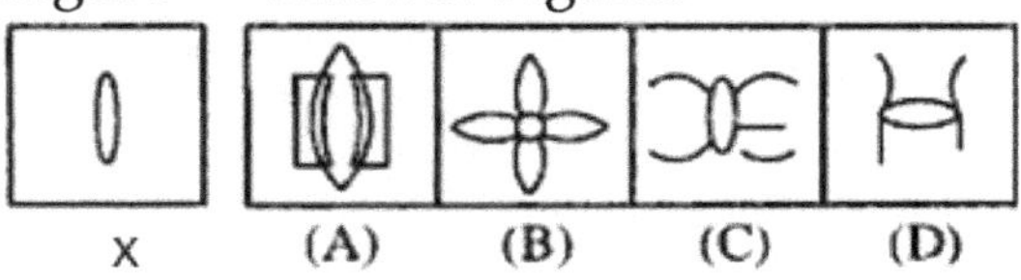

(A) A
(B) B
(C) C
(D) D

27. Find out the alternative figure which contains figure (X) as its part.

Figure   Answer Figures

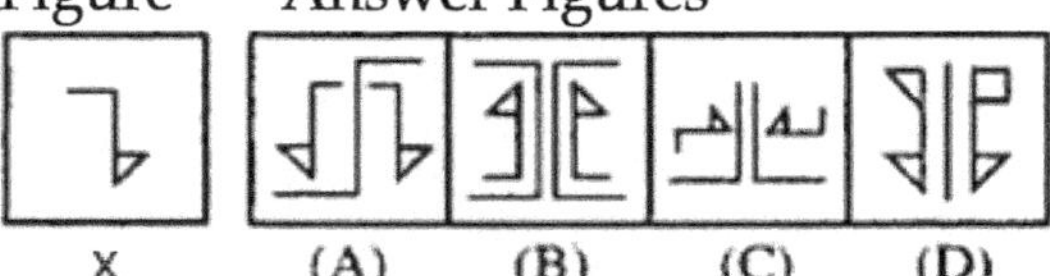

(A) A
(B) B
(C) C
(D) D

28. Select a suitable figure from the four alternatives to make the figure matrix complete.

Matrix   Answer Figures

(A) A
(B) B
(C) C
(D) D

29. Select a suitable figure from the four alternatives to make the figure matrix complete.

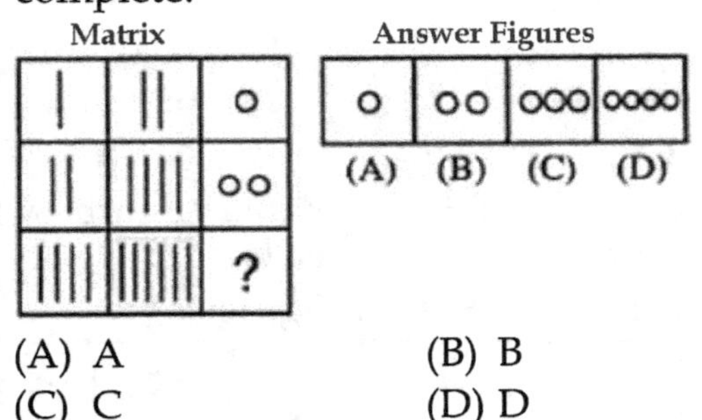

(A) A
(B) B
(C) C
(D) D

30. Select a suitable figure from the four alternatives to make the figure matrix complete.

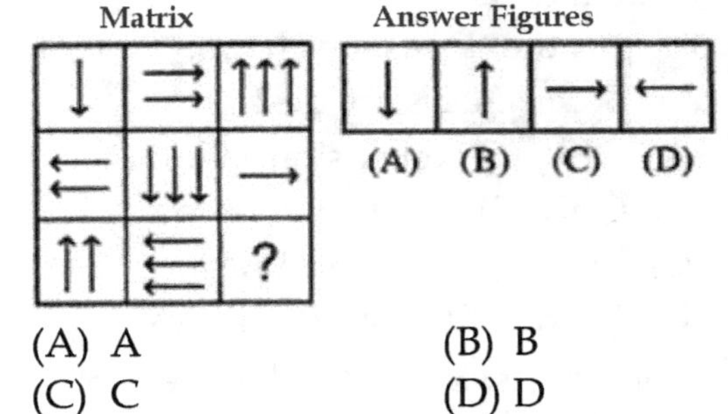

(A) A
(B) B
(C) C
(D) D

1.	Ⓐ Ⓑ Ⓒ Ⓓ	7.	Ⓐ Ⓑ Ⓒ Ⓓ	13.	Ⓐ Ⓑ Ⓒ Ⓓ	19.	Ⓐ Ⓑ Ⓒ Ⓓ	25.	Ⓐ Ⓑ Ⓒ Ⓓ
2.	Ⓐ Ⓑ Ⓒ Ⓓ	8.	Ⓐ Ⓑ Ⓒ Ⓓ	14.	Ⓐ Ⓑ Ⓒ Ⓓ	20.	Ⓐ Ⓑ Ⓒ Ⓓ	26.	Ⓐ Ⓑ Ⓒ Ⓓ
3.	Ⓐ Ⓑ Ⓒ Ⓓ	9.	Ⓐ Ⓑ Ⓒ Ⓓ	15.	Ⓐ Ⓑ Ⓒ Ⓓ	21.	Ⓐ Ⓑ Ⓒ Ⓓ	27.	Ⓐ Ⓑ Ⓒ Ⓓ
4.	Ⓐ Ⓑ Ⓒ Ⓓ	10.	Ⓐ Ⓑ Ⓒ Ⓓ	16.	Ⓐ Ⓑ Ⓒ Ⓓ	22.	Ⓐ Ⓑ Ⓒ Ⓓ	28.	Ⓐ Ⓑ Ⓒ Ⓓ
5.	Ⓐ Ⓑ Ⓒ Ⓓ	11.	Ⓐ Ⓑ Ⓒ Ⓓ	17.	Ⓐ Ⓑ Ⓒ Ⓓ	23.	Ⓐ Ⓑ Ⓒ Ⓓ	29.	Ⓐ Ⓑ Ⓒ Ⓓ
6.	Ⓐ Ⓑ Ⓒ Ⓓ	12.	Ⓐ Ⓑ Ⓒ Ⓓ	18.	Ⓐ Ⓑ Ⓒ Ⓓ	24.	Ⓐ Ⓑ Ⓒ Ⓓ	30.	Ⓐ Ⓑ Ⓒ Ⓓ

MODEL TEST PAPER

MULTIPLE CHOICE QUESTIONS

1. How many unit cubes were added to the solid on the left to obtain the solid on the right?

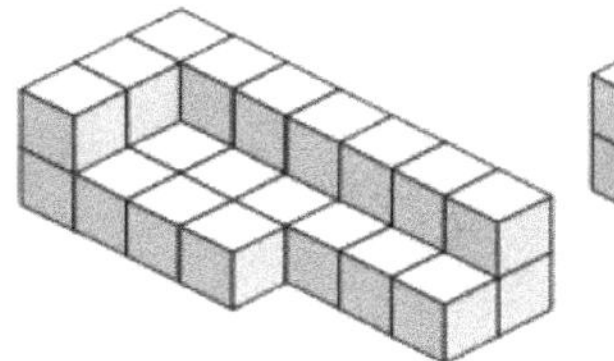 

   (A) 14   (B) 12
   (C) 28   (D) 10

2. Mohit is facing the police post. Where will he be facing if he turns 270° clockwise and then 135° anticlockwise?

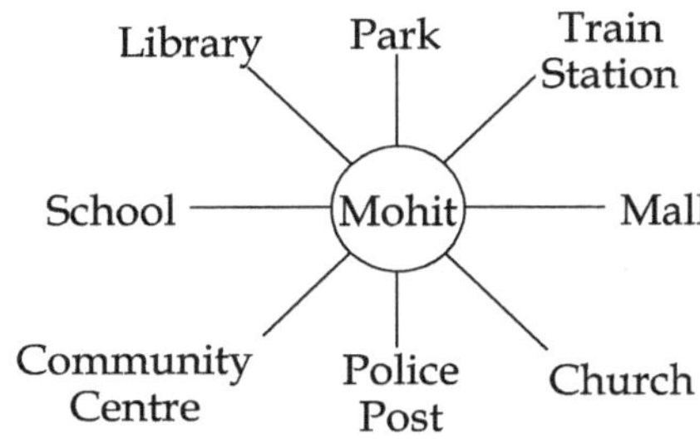

   (A) Library   (B) School
   (C) Train Station   (D) Mall

3. Find the missing letter.
   A, Z, X, B, V, T, C, R, ?, ?
   (A) P, D
   (B) E, O
   (C) Q, E
   (D) O, Q

4. If the first half of the English alphabet is reversed and then next portion of English alphabet is reversed so as 'A' takes the position of 'M' and 'N' takes the position of 'Z' in English alphabet series, then which letter will be 6th to the left of 17th letter to the right of 7th letter from the left end?
   (A) U
   (B) V
   (C) C
   (D) D

5. Which of the following nets can be used to form the dice given below?

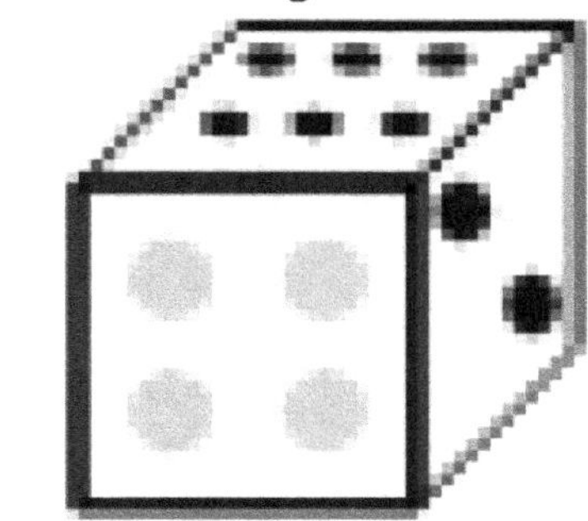

   (A) 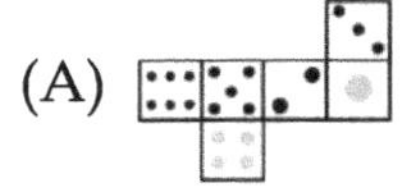   (B) 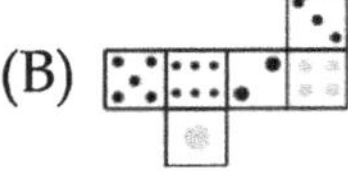

   (C) 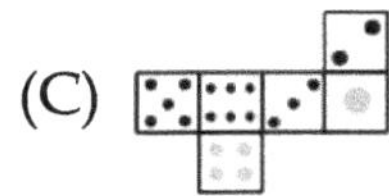   (D) 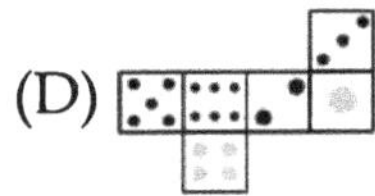

6. If 'REQUEST' is written as 'S2R52TU', then how will 'ACID' be written?
   (A) BDJE
   (B) 1394
   (C) B3J4
   (D) 1D3E

7. Rohit scored more marks than Tarun but less than Kabir. Raj scored more than Vansh but less than Harshit. Kabir scored less than Vansh. Who scored the highest marks?

(A) Kabir
(B) Harshit
(C) Raj
(D) Vansh

8. If P is brother of Q and R is sister of Q, then how is Q related to P?

(A) Uncle
(B) Father
(C) Brother
(D) Cannot be determined

9. In the given figure, the triangle represents girls, the square represents players and the circle represents married. The portion in the figure which represents girls, who are players but not married is labelled as ______.

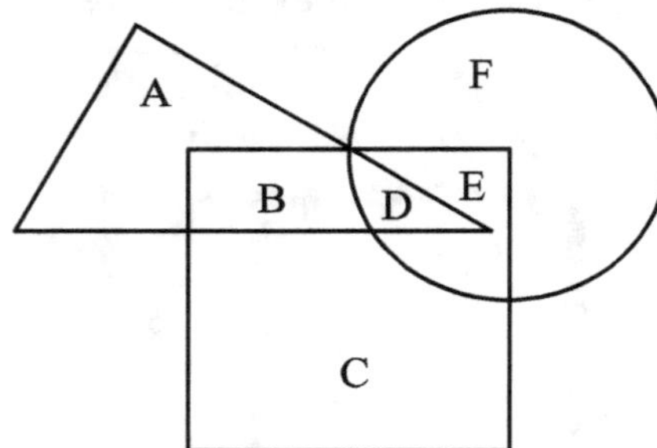

(A) A
(B) B
(C) D
(D) E

10. If the positions of the first and second digits are interchanged, then which of the following will be third if they are arranged in ascending order?

972 526 487 359 251

(A) 359
(B) 972
(C) 526
(D) 487

11. When was the world's first laptop introduced in market and by which company?

(A) Epson, 1981
(B) IBM, 1950
(C) Microsoft, 1988
(D) Compaq, 1965

12. First digital computer built with IC chips was known as ______.

(A) IBM 7090
(B) Apple-1
(C) IBM system/360
(D) Vax-10

13. Which was the world first minicomputer?

(A) PDP-I
(B) IBM system/36
(C) PDP-II
(D) Vax 11/780

14. Punched card used ______.

(A) Alphanumeric code
(B) Hollerith code
(C) EBCDIC code
(D) ASCII code

15. The first computer made available for commercial use was ______.

(A) Mark-I
(B) ENAIC
(C) EDSAC
(D) UNIVAC

16. Internet works on ______.

(A) Packet switching
(B) Circuit switching
(C) Both packet switching and circuit switching
(D) None of these

17. Which one of the following is not an application layer protocol used in internet?

(A) Remote procedure call
(B) Internet relay chat
(C) Resource reservation protocol
(D) None of these

18. Which one of the following is not used in media access control?

(A) Ethernet
(B) Digital subscriber line
(C) Fiber distributed data interface

OLYMPIAD WORKBOOK (NCO) CLASS— 6

(d) Packet Switching

19. In Microsoft PowerPoint, two kinds of sound effects files that can be added to the presentation are __________.
    (A) .wav files and .mid files
    (B) .wav files and .gif files
    (C) .wav files and .jpg files
    (D) .jpg files and .gif files

20. What is a slide-title master pair?
    (A) The title area and text area of a specific slide
    (B) A slide master and title master merged into a single slide
    (C) A slide master and title master for a specific design template
    (D) All of these

21. A motion sensing input device by Microsoft for Xbox 360 video game console and Windows PC is ______.
    (A) Optical mouse
    (B) Kinect
    (C) Joystick
    (D) Touchpad

22. You have to insert your school logo, your name and your class on all slides of your presentation in MS PowerPoint. How should you make sure that the information is added to all slides?
    (A) Add this information in the first slide. Then, whenever you add a new slide, this information will be added to that slide automatically.
    (B) Add this information to the slide master. It will be included in all the slides in the presentation.
    (C) Add this information in the slide layout. It will be included on all slides.
    (D) All of these are correct.

23. What is x86?
    (A) It is a type of networking protocol.
    (B) It is a type of a computer processor.
    (C) It is name for a type of a RAM.
    (D) It is a name of a 4GL.

24. Your school library has different types of printers connected to the school computer. One day only one printer was working and the others were being serviced. The only working printer failed to print. You called library assistant for some help, and, he did something and it printed the page correctly.

    What did the assistant do such that the story was printed correctly?
    (A) He might have rebooted the computer.
    (B) He selected the functional printer in the print dialog.
    (C) He rebooted the printer.
    (D) None of these

25. Which of the following is an incorrect syntax for the PRINT statement in QBASIC?
    (i) PRINT "text/message"
    (ii) PRINT "text", <any number>
    (iii) PRINT <any number>
    (iv) PRINT "text"; <any number>
    (v) PRINT
    (A) (iv) is incorrect
    (B) (v) is incorrect
    (C) (i) and (ii) are incorrect
    (D) All of these are correct

26. Match the following.

Column-I	Column-II
(i) PRINT 4 + 5	(a) 1
(ii) PRINT 16 MOD 3	(b) 256
(iii) PRINT 55\11	(c) 9
(iv) PRINT 4^4	(d) 48
(v) PRINT 16*3	(e) 5

    (A) (i)–(c), (ii)–(d), (iii)–(e), (iv)–(b), (v)–(a)

(B) (i)–(c), (ii)–(a), (iii)–(e), (iv)–(b), (v)–(d)
(C) (i)–(c), (ii)–(e), (iii)–(a), (iv)–(b), (v)–(d)
(D) (i)–(c), (ii)–(a), (iii)–(b), (iv)–(c), (v)–(d)

27. Which of the following devices is used for printing high-quality graphics, charts, tables and diagrams?

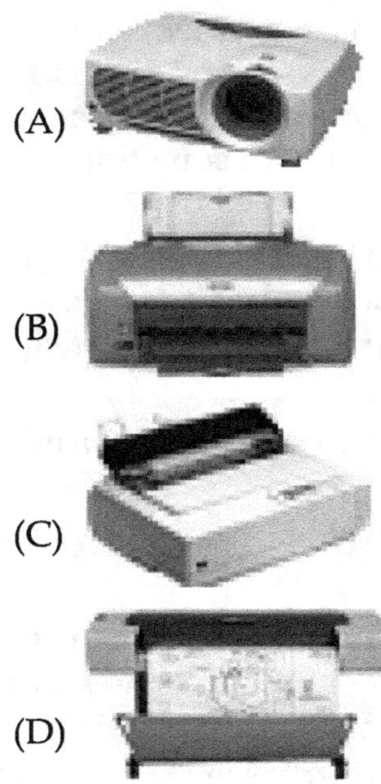

(A)

(B)

(C)

(D)

28. Pratik has created a document in MS Word. He has referred several books and periodicals while creating the document. He now wants to enter names of sources which he has referred to at the end of the document, with proper references to the same in the body of the document. Which of the following should he use?
(A) Footnote
(B) Endnote
(C) Footer
(D) TOC

29. Find the odd one out.
(A) www.peopleinders.com
(B) www.facebook.com
(C) www.google.com
(D) www.anywho.com

30. Given below is a business card which contains a graphical image called the QR-code. What does the QR-code on the card signify?

(A) The QR-code is the logo of the company. They are into the business of generating QR-codes.
(B) The QR-code contains all relevant information about the company and can be stored in the address book of a mobile device having a QR-code reader.
(C) The QR-code contains a coded logo of the organization.
(D) None of these

31. Which of the following is NOT a spreadsheet package?
(A) Lotus 1-2-3   (B) Sybase
(C) Quattro Pro   (D) WingZ

32. Which of the following is NOT an advantage of MICR?
(A) Documents prepared for MICR are difficult to forge.
(B) Banks can process millions of cheques with 100% accuracy.
(C) It can read data even if the document is smudged or crumbled.
(D) It is suitable for inputting large amounts of data.

33. See the characteristics mentioned below.
(i) A fast method of inputting large amount of data.

(ii) Only suitable for recording one out of a selection of answers.

(iii) Only one computer needed to collect and process the data.

(iv) Used in processing Lotto tickets and surveys.

These characteristics are of a/an ______.

(A) OCR

(B) OMR

(C) MICR

(D) Barcode reader

34. Name the input device shown below.

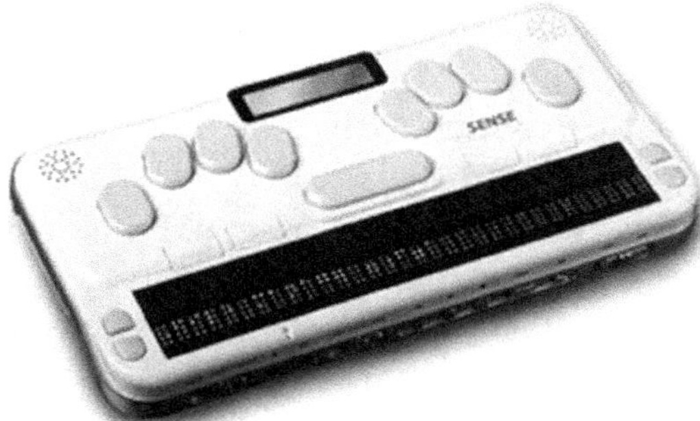

(A) Wireless mouse

(B) Ergonomic keyboard

(C) Braille keyboard

(D) Joystick

35. The first digital computer capable of displaying real time text and graphics on video terminal, which was a large oscilloscope screen, was ________.

(A) Apple I

(B) Whirlwind

(C) Mark I

(D) Cray-I

36. Which of the following is the first commercial computer to use GUI?

(A) Lisa

(B) Altair 8800

(C) Apple II

(D) Cray-II

37. Identify the given logo.

(A) Reddit

(B) Ddig

(C) Twitter

(D) Tweetmeme

38. Which of the following is NOT a valid name of a variable in QBASIC?

(A) LETA$

(B) a%b_c

(C) a$b%

(D) a12$

39. DVD+R DL is a type of DVD that provides ________.

(A) Two recordable dye layers on a single sided disc

(B) Multiple recordable layers on a double sided disc

(C) One layer to be recorded twice

(D) Both (B) and (C)

40. Woxi Media SmartPod is a device recently launched that ______.

(A) Allows user to browse internet, download apps, play games on TV

(B) Is both a tablet and smartphone

(C) Can be connected to desktop to watch TV

(D) Is an mp3 player used to listen to music

41. A technology by which a user can view a media file in real time, without having to wait for it to be downloaded is _________.

(A) Video streaming
(B) Video conferencing
(C) Video uploading
(D) Realtime video

42. Which of the following is used to change the position, size and formatting of the slide placeholders to their default settings in MS PowerPoint?

(A) 

(B) 

(C) 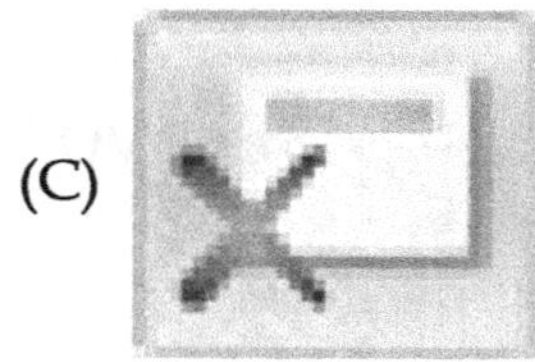

(D) 

43. Which of the following is NOT a function of Personalization in Control Panel of Windows?

(A) Change the themes and sounds on your computer.
(B) Change your account picture
(C) Customize start menu
(D) Text and descriptions read aloud.

44. In MS Word, Ctrl+5 keyboard shortcut key _________.

(A) Sets 1.5 line spacing
(B) Sets 5 line spacing
(C) Saves the document
(D) Justifies the text

45. Mrs. Pandey, your class teacher is creating a time-table in MS Word. She is using tables to create the time-table. While entering names of days, she wishes if those could be in title case, i.e. the first character of the name be in a capital letter, and that may be done automatically as she types. You tell Mrs. Pandey that there is a MS Word feature which will help her meet this requirement.

How would you help her set this feature in MS Word?

(A) Review → AutoCorrect options → Capitalize names of days
(B) Select Capitalize → Each Word from Change Case
(C) File → Options → Proofing → Auto Correct options → Capitalize names of days
(D) MS-Word does not support this option

46. _________ is a minicomputer, _________ is a mainframe computer and _________ is a supercomputer respectively.

(A) CDC 160A, IBM zEnterprise, Cray-1
(B) Cray-1, CDC 160A, IBM zEnterprise
(C) CDC 160A, Cray-1, IBM zEnterprise
(D) IBM zEnterprise, CDC 160A, Cray-1

47. Portable printers usually use _________ printing method.

(A) Laser
(B) Dot-matrix
(C) Inkjet
(D) None of these

48. Duo, Pro-HG, Pro Duo are different varieties of a _______.
   (A) Zip Disk
   (B) CD
   (C) DVD
   (D) Memory Stick

49. MRAM is a type of RAM that retains data even after power supply is cut off, what does 'M' stand for?
   (A) Magnetic
   (B) Magneto resistive
   (C) Magnified
   (D) Mobile

50. What is "pointer trail" feature used for in mouse configuration?
   (A) It helps you select pointer shape of your choice.
   (B) It helps you track mouse cursors more efficiently on small screens.
   (C) It helps in changing the speed of mouse pointer.
   (D) None of these

Darken Your Choice with HB Pencil

1.	Ⓐ Ⓑ Ⓒ Ⓓ	11.	Ⓐ Ⓑ Ⓒ Ⓓ	21.	Ⓐ Ⓑ Ⓒ Ⓓ	31.	Ⓐ Ⓑ Ⓒ Ⓓ	41.	Ⓐ Ⓑ Ⓒ Ⓓ
2.	Ⓐ Ⓑ Ⓒ Ⓓ	12.	Ⓐ Ⓑ Ⓒ Ⓓ	22.	Ⓐ Ⓑ Ⓒ Ⓓ	32.	Ⓐ Ⓑ Ⓒ Ⓓ	42.	Ⓐ Ⓑ Ⓒ Ⓓ
3.	Ⓐ Ⓑ Ⓒ Ⓓ	13.	Ⓐ Ⓑ Ⓒ Ⓓ	23.	Ⓐ Ⓑ Ⓒ Ⓓ	33.	Ⓐ Ⓑ Ⓒ Ⓓ	43.	Ⓐ Ⓑ Ⓒ Ⓓ
4.	Ⓐ Ⓑ Ⓒ Ⓓ	14.	Ⓐ Ⓑ Ⓒ Ⓓ	24.	Ⓐ Ⓑ Ⓒ Ⓓ	34.	Ⓐ Ⓑ Ⓒ Ⓓ	44.	Ⓐ Ⓑ Ⓒ Ⓓ
5.	Ⓐ Ⓑ Ⓒ Ⓓ	15.	Ⓐ Ⓑ Ⓒ Ⓓ	25.	Ⓐ Ⓑ Ⓒ Ⓓ	35.	Ⓐ Ⓑ Ⓒ Ⓓ	45.	Ⓐ Ⓑ Ⓒ Ⓓ
6.	Ⓐ Ⓑ Ⓒ Ⓓ	16.	Ⓐ Ⓑ Ⓒ Ⓓ	26.	Ⓐ Ⓑ Ⓒ Ⓓ	36.	Ⓐ Ⓑ Ⓒ Ⓓ	46.	Ⓐ Ⓑ Ⓒ Ⓓ
7.	Ⓐ Ⓑ Ⓒ Ⓓ	17.	Ⓐ Ⓑ Ⓒ Ⓓ	27.	Ⓐ Ⓑ Ⓒ Ⓓ	37.	Ⓐ Ⓑ Ⓒ Ⓓ	47.	Ⓐ Ⓑ Ⓒ Ⓓ
8.	Ⓐ Ⓑ Ⓒ Ⓓ	18.	Ⓐ Ⓑ Ⓒ Ⓓ	28.	Ⓐ Ⓑ Ⓒ Ⓓ	38.	Ⓐ Ⓑ Ⓒ Ⓓ	48.	Ⓐ Ⓑ Ⓒ Ⓓ
9.	Ⓐ Ⓑ Ⓒ Ⓓ	19.	Ⓐ Ⓑ Ⓒ Ⓓ	29.	Ⓐ Ⓑ Ⓒ Ⓓ	39.	Ⓐ Ⓑ Ⓒ Ⓓ	49.	Ⓐ Ⓑ Ⓒ Ⓓ
10.	Ⓐ Ⓑ Ⓒ Ⓓ	20.	Ⓐ Ⓑ Ⓒ Ⓓ	30.	Ⓐ Ⓑ Ⓒ Ⓓ	40.	Ⓐ Ⓑ Ⓒ Ⓓ	50.	Ⓐ Ⓑ Ⓒ Ⓓ

1. FUNDAMENTALS OF COMPUTER

Answer Key

1. (B)	2. (D)	3. (A)	4. (D)	5. (A)	6. (C)	7. (D)	8. (D)	9. (B)	10. (A)
11. (D)	12. (D)	13. (A)	14. (B)	15. (D)	16. (B)	17. (C)	18. (D)	19. (A)	20. (D)

HOTS (ACHIEVERS SECTION)

21. (D)	22. (D)	23. (A)	24. (D)	25. (B)

2. MEMORY AND STORAGE DEVICES

Answer Key

1. (D)	2. (A)	3. (A)	4. (D)	5. (D)	6. (C)	7. (A)	8. (D)	9. (D)	10. (B)
11. (B)	12. (C)	13. (C)	14. (D)	15. (B)	16. (C)	17. (D)	18. (C)	19. (C)	20. (B)

2. (A)

In computer storage media, WORM (write once, read many) is a data storage technology that allows information to be written to a disc a single time and prevents the drive from erasing the data.

3. (A)

Examples of secondary storage are: CDs, DVs, pendrive, etc.

4. (D)

Option (D) is of RAM (Random Access Memory), which is a primary memory of a computer.

9. (D)

PATA and SATA are both types of hard drive connections. PATA stands for parallel ATA, and SATA stands for serial ATA.

11. (B)

Example of volatile memory is RAM and example of non-volatile memory are hard disk, CDs, etc.

15. (B)

Dynamic random access memory (DRAM) is a type of memory that is typically used for data or program code that a computer processor needs to function. DRAM is a common type of random access memory (RAM) used in personal computers (PCs), workstations and servers. It needs to be refreshed periodically.

20. (B)

A solid-state drive (SSD) is a non-volatile storage device that stores persistent data on solid-state flash memory.

| 21. (B) | 22. (A) | 23. (D) | 24. (C) | 25. (A) |

21. (B)

The computer processes and stores data and instructions in the form of two digits that is 0's and 1. This digits (i.e is 0's and 1 are called as Binary digits or Bits) . In computer memory, a Bit is a very small unit of information that any computer can process or store.

22. (A)

PROM stands for Programmable Read Only Memory. It is a blank chip which is used to store the contents/ data and instructions i.e too permanently. For writing programs on the blank PROM chips, the programmers make use of microcode instructions.

23. (D)

The full abbreviation of EPROM is Erasable Programmable Read Only Memory. It is the one type of ROM chip, on which the contents are stored and erased with the help of making use of ultraviolet light. Once the contents are erased/removed from the ROM chip, then they are reprogrammed by using PROM program.

3. EVOLUTION OF COMPUTER

Answer Key

1. (B)	2. (B)	3. (B)	4. (C)	5. (A)	6. (C)	7. (C)	8. (D)	9. (A)	10. (A)
11. (D)	12. (D)	13. (D)	14. (C)	15. (C)	16. (D)	17. (A)	18. (A)	19. (D)	20. (B)

HOTS (ACHIEVERS SECTION)

| 21. (C) | 22. (A) | 23. (D) | 24. (C) | 25. (D) |

4. WINDOWS 10

Answer Key

1. (A)	2. (D)	3. (C)	4. (D)	5. (A)	6. (D)	7. (C)	8. (A)	9. (A)	10. (C)
11. (C)	12. (A)	13. (C)	14. (D)	15. (A)	16. (C)	17. (B)	18. (A)	19. (B)	20. (A)

HOTS (ACHIEVERS SECTION)

| 21. (D) | 22. (A) | 23. (C) | 24. (D) | 25. (A) |

5. MS WORD

Answer Key

1. (B)	2. (D)	3. (A)	4. (B)	5. (A)	6. (B)	7. (D)	8. (A)	9. (A)	10. (B)
11. (D)	12. (B)	13. (A)	14. (A)	15. (D)	16. (B)	17. (D)	18. (A)	19. (D)	20. (C)

HOTS (ACHIEVERS SECTION)

21. (A)	22. (D)	23. (A)	24. (B)	25. (B)

6. MS POWERPOINT

Answer Key

1. (C)	2. (D)	3. (D)	4. (A)	5. (B)	6. (A)	7. (B)	8. (A)	9. (B)	10. (C)
11. (A)	12. (C)	13. (C)	14. (D)	15. (C)	16. (C)	17. (B)	18. (A)	19. (D)	20. (D)

HOTS (ACHIEVERS SECTION)

21. (B)	22. (C)	23. (D)	24. (D)	25. (A)

7. INTRODUCTION TO QBASIC

Answer Key

1. (C)	2. (A)	3. (B)	4. (D)	5. (C)	6. (A)	7. (A)	8. (A)	9. (B)	10. (A)
11. (D)	12. (A)	13. (B)	14. (B)	15. (A)	16. (B)	17. (C)	18. (D)	19. (B)	20. (D)

HOTS (ACHIEVERS SECTION)

21. (B)	22. (A)	23. (A)	24. (C)	25. (B)

8. INTERNET AND E-MAIL

Answer Key

1. (B)	2. (B)	3. (C)	4. (B)	5. (A)	6. (C)	7. (D)	8. (D)	9. (B)	10. (A)
11. (C)	12. (B)	13. (B)	14. (B)	15. (B)	16. (B)	17. (B)	18. (C)	19. (C)	20. (C)

HOTS (ACHIEVERS SECTION)

21. (B)	22. (D)	23. (B)	24. (D)	25. (A)

OLYMPIAD WORKBOOK (NCO) CLASS— 6

Answer Key

1. (B)	2. (D)	3. (B)	4. (C)	5. (A)	6. (D)	7. (B)	8. (D)	9. (D)	10. (C)
11. (B)	12. (D)	13. (C)	14. (A)	15. (D)	16. (D)	17. (C)	18. (C)	19. (B)	20. (C)

HOTS (ACHIEVERS SECTION)

21. (A)	22. (D)	23. (B)	24. (B)	25. (B)

10. LOGICAL REASONING

Answer Key

1. (A)	2. (C)	3. (C)	4. (B)	5. (C)	6. (C)	7. (A)	8. (C)	9. (C)	10. (D)
11. (A)	12. (C)	13. (A)	14. (B)	15. (D)	16. (D)	17. (D)	18. (B)	19. (B)	20. (D)
21. (B)	22. (D)	23. (A)	24. (B)	25. (C)	26. (C)	27. (A)	28. (D)	29. (D)	30. (A)

7. (A)

The series is mopn/mopn/mopn/mopn. Thus, the pattern 'mopn' is repeated.

8. (B)

The series is bbccaa/ccaabb/aabbcc. Thus, the letter pairs move in a cyclic order.

9. (C)

The series is man/man/man/man/man. Thus, the pattern 'man' is repeated.

10. (D)

Because, wife of husband - herself; Brother of daughter - son. So, the man is Ritu's son.

11. (A)

Grandmother is one female, mother is another female, the wives of four sons are four females and two daughters of all four sons are eight females. So, in all there are $1 + 1 + 4 + 8 = 14$ females.

12. (C)

Shalu is Mona's step-daughter, which means Shalu is the daughter of the other wife of Ravi. So, Shalu is the daughter of Leena.

MODEL TEST PAPER

Answer Key

1. (A)	2. (A)	3. (A)	4. (B)	5. (D)	6. (D)	7. (B)	8. (D)	9. (B)	10. (A)
11. (A)	12. (C)	13. (A)	14. (B)	15. (D)	16. (A)	17. (C)	18. (D)	19. (A)	20. (A)
21. (B)	22. (B)	23. (B)	24. (B)	25. (D)	26. (B)	27. (D)	28. (B)	29. (C)	30. (B)
31. (B)	32. (C)	33. (B)	34. (C)	35. (B)	36. (A)	37. (A)	38. (B)	39. (A)	40. (A)
41. (A)	42. (B)	43. (D)	44. (A)	45. (C)	46. (A)	47. (C)	48. (D)	49. (B)	50. (B)

SAMPLE OMR ANSWER SHEET

1. STUDENT NAME (IN ENGLISH CAPITAL LETTERS ONLY)

Students must write and darken the respective circles completely using HB Pencil only. Othewise their Answer Sheets will not be evaluated.

PERSONAL DETAILS

2. SCHOOL CODE

3. CLASS

4. SECTION

5. ROLL NO.

6. QUESTION PAPER SET

A ○
B ○
C ○
D ○

7. MOBILE NUMBER

8. GENDER

MALE ○
FEMALE ○

9. STREAM
(Only for Class XI and XII Students)

MATHEMATICS ○
BIOLOGY ○
OTHERS ○

MARK YOUR ANSWERS

No.	A	B	C	D	No.	A	B	C	D
1.	Ⓐ	Ⓑ	Ⓒ	Ⓓ	26.	Ⓐ	Ⓑ	Ⓒ	Ⓓ
2.	Ⓐ	Ⓑ	Ⓒ	Ⓓ	27.	Ⓐ	Ⓑ	Ⓒ	Ⓓ
3.	Ⓐ	Ⓑ	Ⓒ	Ⓓ	28.	Ⓐ	Ⓑ	Ⓒ	Ⓓ
4.	Ⓐ	Ⓑ	Ⓒ	Ⓓ	29.	Ⓐ	Ⓑ	Ⓒ	Ⓓ
5.	Ⓐ	Ⓑ	Ⓒ	Ⓓ	30.	Ⓐ	Ⓑ	Ⓒ	Ⓓ
6.	Ⓐ	Ⓑ	Ⓒ	Ⓓ	31.	Ⓐ	Ⓑ	Ⓒ	Ⓓ
7.	Ⓐ	Ⓑ	Ⓒ	Ⓓ	32.	Ⓐ	Ⓑ	Ⓒ	Ⓓ
8.	Ⓐ	Ⓑ	Ⓒ	Ⓓ	33.	Ⓐ	Ⓑ	Ⓒ	Ⓓ
9.	Ⓐ	Ⓑ	Ⓒ	Ⓓ	34.	Ⓐ	Ⓑ	Ⓒ	Ⓓ
10.	Ⓐ	Ⓑ	Ⓒ	Ⓓ	35.	Ⓐ	Ⓑ	Ⓒ	Ⓓ
11.	Ⓐ	Ⓑ	Ⓒ	Ⓓ	36.	Ⓐ	Ⓑ	Ⓒ	Ⓓ
12.	Ⓐ	Ⓑ	Ⓒ	Ⓓ	37.	Ⓐ	Ⓑ	Ⓒ	Ⓓ
13.	Ⓐ	Ⓑ	Ⓒ	Ⓓ	38.	Ⓐ	Ⓑ	Ⓒ	Ⓓ
14.	Ⓐ	Ⓑ	Ⓒ	Ⓓ	39.	Ⓐ	Ⓑ	Ⓒ	Ⓓ
15.	Ⓐ	Ⓑ	Ⓒ	Ⓓ	40.	Ⓐ	Ⓑ	Ⓒ	Ⓓ
16.	Ⓐ	Ⓑ	Ⓒ	Ⓓ	41.	Ⓐ	Ⓑ	Ⓒ	Ⓓ
17.	Ⓐ	Ⓑ	Ⓒ	Ⓓ	42.	Ⓐ	Ⓑ	Ⓒ	Ⓓ
18.	Ⓐ	Ⓑ	Ⓒ	Ⓓ	43.	Ⓐ	Ⓑ	Ⓒ	Ⓓ
19.	Ⓐ	Ⓑ	Ⓒ	Ⓓ	44.	Ⓐ	Ⓑ	Ⓒ	Ⓓ
20.	Ⓐ	Ⓑ	Ⓒ	Ⓓ	45.	Ⓐ	Ⓑ	Ⓒ	Ⓓ
21.	Ⓐ	Ⓑ	Ⓒ	Ⓓ	46.	Ⓐ	Ⓑ	Ⓒ	Ⓓ
22.	Ⓐ	Ⓑ	Ⓒ	Ⓓ	47.	Ⓐ	Ⓑ	Ⓒ	Ⓓ
23.	Ⓐ	Ⓑ	Ⓒ	Ⓓ	48.	Ⓐ	Ⓑ	Ⓒ	Ⓓ
24.	Ⓐ	Ⓑ	Ⓒ	Ⓓ	49.	Ⓐ	Ⓑ	Ⓒ	Ⓓ
25.	Ⓐ	Ⓑ	Ⓒ	Ⓓ	50.	Ⓐ	Ⓑ	Ⓒ	Ⓓ

Signature of the Student & Date of Examination

Signature of the Invigilator & Date of Examination

V&S Publishers, F-2/16 Ansari Road, Daryaganj, New Delhi-110002, ☎ 011-23240026-27
✉ info@vspublishers.com, ⊕ www.vspublishers.com